ALL NEW 100 LITERACY HOURS

- Differentiated lesson plans
- Photocopiable extracts
- Covers the Early Learning Goals and NLS objectives

YEAR 3

James Friel, Gill Friel and Sue Ellis

CREDITS

Authors
James Friel
Gill Friel
Sue Ellis

Illustrations
Beverly Curl

Editor
Roanne Charles

Series Designer
Joy Monkhouse

Assistant Editor
Victoria Paley

Designers
Erik Ivens &
Melissa Leek

Text © James Friel, Gill Friel and Sue Ellis
© 2005 Scholastic Ltd

Designed using Adobe InDesign

Published by Scholastic Ltd
Villiers House
Clarendon Avenue
Leamington Spa
Warwickshire CV32 5PR

www.scholastic.co.uk

Printed by Bell and Bain Ltd, Glasgow.

2 3 4 5 6 7 8 9   5 6 7 8 9 0 1 2 3 4

ACKNOWLEDGEMENTS

The publishers gratefully acknowledge permission to reproduce the following copyright material: **Nicola Bayley** for the use of an illustration from *Read and Respond: The Mousehole Cat* by Sylvia Karavis and Catherine Byrne, based on *The Mousehole Cat* by Antonia Barber ©1998, Nicola Bayley (1998, Scholastic Limited). **Carcanet Press Limited** for the use of 'The Loch Ness Monster's Song' by Edwin Morgan from *Collected Poems* by Edwin Morgan © 1990, Edwin Morgan (1990, Carcanet Press). **Carlton Publishing Group** for the use of an extract from 'Adventures of Isabel' by Ogden Nash from *Verses from 1929 onwards* by Ogden Nash © 1959, Ogden Nash (1959, Dent). **Peggy Cotton** for 'Listen' by John Cotton from *The Crystal Zoo* by John Cotton, L J Anderson and U A Fanthorpe © 1985, John Cotton (1985, Oxford University Press). **Curtis Brown Limited** for the use of 'Wha Me Mudder Do' by Grace Nichols from *Poetry Jump Up* edited by Grace Nichols © 1990, Grace Nichols (1990, Puffin). **Egmont Books Limited** for the use of extracts from *Flat Stanley* by Jeff Brown © 1964, Jeff Brown (1964, Egmont Books Limited) and 'The King's Breakfast' from *When We Were Very Young* by A A Milne © 1924, A A Milne (1924, Methuen). **John Foster** for the use of 'The Worries' and 'The Ghost House' by John Foster © 2005, John Foster, previously unpublished. **Trevor Harvey** for use of 'There once was a young boy called Garth' and 'There once was a young girl called Jane' by Trevor Harvey © 2005, Trevor Harvey, previously unpublished. **Trevor Harvey** for the use of 'Heartbeat Chartbeat' by Trevor Harvey from *Loopy Limericks* edited by John Foster © 2001, Trevor Harvey (2001, Collins). **Trevor Harvey** for the use of 'There once was a teacher from Crewe' by Trevor Harvey from *Fiendishly Funny Poems* chosen by John Foster © 2004, Trevor Harvey (2004, Collins). **Libby Houston** for the use of 'Black Dot' by Libby Houston from *All Change: Poems by Libby Houston* © 1993, Libby Houston (1993, Oxford University Press). **Tony Mitton** for the use of 'Forbidden Poem' by Tony Mitton from *Plum* by Tony Mitton © 1998, Tony Mitton (1998, Scholastic Children's Books). **The Penguin Group (UK) Ltd** for the use of 'Talk Us Through It, Charlotte' and 'How To Score Goals' by Allan Ahlberg from *Friendly Matches* by Allan Ahlberg © 2001, Allan Ahlberg (2001, Viking). **The Peters Fraser and Dunlop Group Limited** for the use of 'An Attempt At An Unrhymed Verse' by Wendy Cope from *Overheard on a saltmarsh* edited by Carol Ann Duffy © 2003, Wendy Cope (2003, Young Picador). **The Peters Fraser and Dunlop Group Limited** on behalf of the Estate of Hilaire Belloc for the use of 'Matilda' by Hilaire Belloc from *Cautionary Verses* by Hilaire Belloc © 1930, Estate of Hilaire Belloc (1930, Random House). **The Random House Group** for the use of an extract from *Timid Tim and the Cuggy Thief* by John Prater © 1994, John Prater (1994, Red Fox). **Marian Reiner Literary Agency**, New York for the use of 'Owl of the Greenwood' by Patricia Hubbell from *Catch Me a Wind* by Patricia Hubbell © 1968, 1996 Patricia Hubbell (1968, Antheneum Publishers Inc) **Marian Reiner Literary Agency**, New York for the use of 'For Mugs' by Myrah Cohn Livingston from *4-Way Stop and other poems* by Myra Cohn Livingston © 1976, Myrah Cohn Livingston (1976, Atheneum).

British Library Cataloguing-in-Publication Data
A catalogue record for this book is available from the British Library.

ISBN 0-439-971-675
ISBN 978-0439-9716-76

The right of James Friel, Gill Friel and Sue Ellis to be identified as the authors of this work has been asserted by them in accordance with the Copyright, Designs and Patents Act 1988.

Extracts from The National Literacy Strategy © Crown copyright. Reproduced under the terms of HMSO Guidance Note 8.

Due to the nature of the web, we cannot guarantee the content or links of any sites featured. We strongly recommend that teachers check websites before using them in the classroom.

Post-it is a registered trademark of 3M

Every effort has been made to trace copyright holders for the works reproduced in this book, and the publishers apologise for any inadvertent omissions.

Contents

ALL NEW 100 LITERACY HOURS: YEAR 3

About the series

The books in the updated *All New 100 Literacy Hours* series offer a set of completely new term-by-term lesson plans, complete with objectives and organisation grids and accompanied, where relevant, with photocopiable texts and activity sheets. The series offers a core of material for the teaching of the English curriculum within the structure of the Literacy Hour, but now perfectly matches the recent NLS *Medium-Term Plans*, *Grammar for Writing*, and *Speaking, Listening and Learning* guidelines. The series also builds on current teaching ideas including providing activities to match children's preferred learning styles.

Using this book
The units of work

This book provides 100 literacy hours for Year 3 based on the National Literacy Strategy *Medium-Term Plans*. The lessons form a core scheme of work or they can be used to supplement your existing planning. This core can be extended in several ways. For example, you can:

● Repeat the sequence of lessons, but with different texts. For example, the lessons on *Flat Stanley* could be repeated using a text such as *The Hundred Mile an Hour Dog* by Jeremy Strong.

● Adding additional texts. For example, including your own favourite poems into the poetry reading in Term 2, or using poems from the anthologies that the children have built up during Term 1.

● Giving extra time for allowing children to read and discuss each others' work or for the drafting and redrafting process. This is essential if it is to be done with the thoroughness recommended in NLS exemplification, for example: *Improving Writing: Writing Flier 1*.

● It is also well worth allowing more time for children to celebrate their work by creating special events such as class book launches, visits from writers in other classes or by inviting parents to attend short displays and presentations for the last half hour of the day. It is vital that children see their work read by others and that they talk about the readers' responses. Throughout the book, we have indicated where this might happen, usually about twice a term.

● In addition to the above, tried-and-tested resources from previous schemes of work, other publications, or the original *100 Literacy Hours*, can be used to supplement the new materials.

INTRODUCTION

Organisation of teaching units

Each term is divided into teaching units comprising between five and ten hours. Each of the units cluster the NLS text-, sentence- and word-level objectives. The units are organised as follows:

Unit overview

Introduction

Overview of each unit including ideas for extending units.

Organisation grid

Outlines the key activities for each lesson.

Key assessment opportunities

A bulleted list of key assessment opportunities. These will help you to plan assessment opportunities throughout each unit.

Unit lesson plans

Each unit of lesson plans is written with the following headings:

Objectives

NLS objectives including Speaking and Listening emphases.

What you need

Provides a list of resources required for each lesson.

Shared work

Sets out the shared text-, sentence- and word-level work in each lesson. Some of these objectives are taught discretely, while others are integrated into the theme of the unit as the NLS recommends.

Guided work and Independent work

Every unit contains at least two suggestions for guided work to be used if the lessons plans are re-organised on a rotational basis. The lessons also include ideas for independent group, paired or individual activities. In some units, you may wish to re-organise these, along with the suggestions for guided work, on a rotational basis, for example, when a group set of books is being shared around the class.

Plenary

Sets out what to do in the whole-class plenary session.

Differentiation

Ideas for supporting more or less able children including ideas for peer and other adult support.

Links to the NLS Medium-Term plans

The units provide clear links to the requirements of the NLS *Medium-Term Plans*. Genres are matched exactly with appropriate texts for the age group and the range of objectives covered, as shown on the grid for each term. Some of the word- and sentence-level objectives identified in the *Medium-Term Plans* have been relocated from the specified units to meet the needs of specific texts and the running order of the selected units.

Differentiation

In every lesson plan, suggestions for supporting the less able and stretching the more able are given. However, it is important to use these advisedly as a child may be 'less able' in some aspects of literacy, but 'more able' in others. These suggestions should be applied when appropriate to the individual child and not be automatically given to a predetermined group. Other important considerations are children's different learning styles, and the concept of 'multiple intelligences'. Children also need to experience working individually, in pairs, and in a range of larger groups, organised in different ways to meet different educational objectives. The number of groups will depend on class size, spread of ability and learning style. Try to ensure a balance of gender and personality type in each group, and don't hesitate to separate children who cannot work well together.

Assessment

Each unit includes a list of bullet points to help with ongoing assessment. These are not intended to replace National Curriculum assessment, but represent the 'bottom line' that all the children should have achieved by the end of the unit. If a number of children have failed to achieve satisfactory standards in any of the bulleted areas, then the unit may need to be revisited (with different resources).

Using the photocopiable resources

Where there is instruction to copy material from copyright texts, you must ensure that this is done within the limits of the photocopy licence of your school. If pupils are using their own exercise books or paper for answers, then all photocopiable resources are reuseable.

Usually, the best way to share a resource with the class is to make a display version for an overhead projector or data projector. However, try to avoid this becoming routine. An effective alternative is to sit with the children in a circle and to work with a hard copy of the text and where possible, engage the children with actual books.

Interactive whiteboard use

Permission is granted for those pages marked as photocopiable to be used in this way. Where third party material is used, permission for interactive whiteboard use must be obtained from the copyright holder or their licensor. This information can be found in the acknowledgements at the front of the book.

Annotations

The methodology of analysing texts by annotation is used in this book. Annotations to texts are given in one margin only, without lines pointing to the textual features they describe. This allows the resource to be used both as an exemplar of annotations and as a blank resource. To make blank resources, cover or fold back the annotations when photocopying. The annotations can be used in several ways:
● Write them 'live' on an enlarged version of the blank resource, adding lines from notes to text as appropriate, to demonstrate how to annotate a text.
● Read a text with the annotations covered, discuss key points, then reveal the annotations.
● Annotate the first part of a text for demonstration purposes then ask children to complete the annotations for the rest of the text in the independent session.
● In an independent reading session, give children a jumbled up version of the annotations and ask them to link them to the appropriate text.
● In a plenary session, display the text and notes together, and add lines from notes to text as each point is raised in discussion.

Speaking and listening

When speaking and listening is one of the main focuses of the lessons, links are made to the Primary National Strategy's *Speaking, Listening and Learning* (DfES, 2003), and to the speaking and listening emphases within the *Medium-Term Planner*. These links are also highlighted in the objectives grid through the use of a logo.

Children will use speaking and listening as a process skill in every lesson. To encourage this, particular emphasis is given to children working with 'talk partners'. When a larger group is needed, 'talk partners' can join into fours. Groups of this size are ideal for discussion and collaborative work as they provide a range of opinion and yet are not too large to make full participation difficult. It is important to vary group organisation so that children experience working with different partners with different approaches or abilities.

Creativity

Recent reports have emphasised the importance of creativity and creativity is embedded within many of the lessons in this book. Also encourage creativity by using some of the following ideas:
- Children as 'real writers' - encourage children to see themselves as real writers writing for real purposes. This means giving them a strong sense of audience and purpose, using redrafting techniques and finding a way of 'publishing' completed work.
- Writing journals - encourage the children to write something in their journal every day. This can be anything they like - diary entry, story, poem, exploration of a problem, and so on. This is the one place where grammar, and punctuation do not matter. The aim is to develop writing fluency, as in a free flow between thought and written page.
- First-hand experiences - many NLS writing tasks are responses to texts. Balance this by using stimulating 'real-life' starting points such as visits, visitors, artefacts, and so forth.
- Experimentation - encourage the children to play with ideas, and explore alternatives. Positively encourage them to suggest alternative tasks.
- Writing materials - provide inspiring media such as paper in various colours and sizes; a variety of pens and pencils (felt-tipped pens, calligraphic pens); rulers; scissors; glue; desktop publishing and presentation software; a clip art library; a colour printer.

Learning styles

Researchers have identified three different learning styles: auditory, kinaesthetic and visual. Most children will use a mixture of all three styles, but in some children, one style will predominate. Many lessons in this book offer specific opportunities for different learning styles.

Media and ICT

There have been major advances in media and ICT. We need to give more emphasis to media education and ICT in the primary classroom. This can be done by showing film versions of books and documentaries on non-fiction topics, and by ensuring that, every time writing takes place, at least one group is writing on a word processor and that children take it in turns to do their research via the internet.

NLS OBJECTIVES

Unit	Text level	Sentence level	Word level	No of hours	Text(s)	Links to GfW, S&L	Outcomes
Narrative: setting	1, 8, 9, 11, 12, 15	1, 3, 5, 12	5, 6, 7, 14	5	*The Mousehole Cat* by Antonia Barber; *Harriet's Hare* by Dick King-Smith	GfW 44, S&L 60	Personification poems
Narrative: dialogue	2, 9, 10, 15	2, 4, 6, 7, 8	8, 17, 19	5	Cartoon strips; 'A ghastly, ghostly encounter' by Gill Friel and James Friel	GfW 45-47 S&L 27, 28	Short story analysis; own short scary stories
Plays	4, 5, 14	2, 7, 10	5	5	'The fire', 'A moment in time' by Gill Friel and James Friel	GfW 47, S&L 28, 31, 32	Screenplay; film review
Poetry	6, 7, 8, 9, 12, 13	2, 5, 6	5, 6, 13, 14, 16, 17, 21	10	'Listen' by Joseph Cotton; 'For Mugs' by Myra Cohn Livingston; 'Old Boy' by Neela Mann; 'Heads or Tails?' and 'Charlotte's Dog' by Kit Wright; 'The Loch Ness Monster's Song' by Edwin Morgan; 'The Ghost House' by John Foster; 'Black Dot' by Libby Houston	S&L 26, 29, 31	Newspaper article; group front page
Fact and fiction	16, 17, 22	3, 5, 9, 10	3, 13, 20	5	Range of fiction and non-fiction; book reviews	S&L 27, 31	Biography from research; autobiography
Reports	18, 19, 21, 22	9, 13	4, 10, 13, 14, 15	5	Birdwatchers' reports	GfW 45	Class booklet of reports

Unit	Text level	Sentence level	Word level	No of hours	Text(s)	Links to GfW, S&L	Outcomes
Narrative: themes	2, 3, 4, 7, 8, 9	2, 3, 6, 8	4, 5, 6, 7, 17, 19, 20, 24, 25, 26	10	'The Boy Who Cried Wolf,' 'The Good Samaritan,' 'George and the Dragon', 'Beowulf and Grendel', 'The Sword in the Stone'	S&L 29, 32	Character descriptions; storyboard; modern-day legend
Narrative: plot	1, 2, 5, 6, 7, 9, 10	4	5, 9, 19, 22	5	Cinderella, Snow White	S&L 29, 31, 32	Storytelling; story sequel; modernised story
Poetry	4, 5, 11	1	10, 18, 26	5	'Forbidden Poem' by Tony Mitton; 'The Worries' by John Foster, 'Wha Me Mudder Do' by Grace Nichols; 'Owl of the Greenwood' by Patricia Hubbell; 'Swing, Swing' by William Allingham;	S&L 29, 32	Poetry performances; own lines for poem
Non-fiction: note-taking and instructions	12, 13, 14, 15, 16, 17	9, 19, 11	5, 13, 19, 22, 27	10	Pictorial and textual instructions, information texts on dinosaurs and castles	GfW 13. S&L 27, 31	Paper helicopter from following instructions; notes and condensed text; board game
Formal	17, 20	2, 5	8	5	Product guarantee; complaint correspondence; guide to plain English	S&L 66	Role-play; formal letter; simplified guarantee.

Unit	Text level	Sentence level	Word level	No of hours	Text(s)	Links to GfW, S&L	Outcomes
Narrative: perspective/ character	3, 4, 5, 12	2, 4	13	5	Talk Us Through It, Charlotte by Allan Ahlberg	GfW 15, S&L 36	Character profile; sport commentary; first person account
Narrative: plot	1, 2, 4, 10, 11, 13	1, 4, 6	5, 6, 13, 17	10	Flat Stanley by Jeff Brown; Timid Tim and the Cuggy Thief by John Prater	GfW 16, 18, S&L 18, 28, 29, 32, 36	Story sequel; oral and written scary/mystery story
Poetry	6, 7, 15, 21	1	14, 17, 19	5	Limericks; humorous poems; alliterative poems; funny story poems	S&L 29	'Poetry wall' anthology; genre poems; poetry performances
Authors	1, 8, 9, 14, 17	5	6	5	Biography of Colin McNaughton; author websites; series fiction		Mini reading journal; book reviews
Note-taking and letters	16, 20, 21, 22, 23, 25, 26	1, 6	5, 19	5	'School in the 1920s'; letters/e-mails	GfW 18, S&L 33	Letters; reports
Alphabetical text	14, 17, 18, 21, 24	7		5	Local directories; information posters; guides giving recommendations/listings	S&L 25	Information poster; Good Read Guide

UNIT 1

Narrative: setting

At the beginning of this unit pupils study two examples of setting by famous writers; they look at the relationship between illustrator and writer and publish a very simple story. Children are introduced to the difference between *telling* about a setting and *showing* a setting. They are taught about the importance of leaving out unimportant detail when writing final drafts.

There are sophisticated ideas introduced and discussed in this unit. Many confident readers and writers at this age are able to access advanced concepts about setting and the earlier the ideas are introduced then the more often they can be referred to when children are reading and writing. There is an emphasis upon punctuation and paragraph construction. Children correct spellings and test one another.

Hour	Shared text-level work	Shared word-/ sentence-level work	Guided and independent work	Plenary
1 Story settings	Exploring story structure; reading two descriptions of story settings.	Using grammar and context to help with new vocabulary.	Exploring setting descriptions; choosing setting descriptions from current reading.	Sharing examples of settings.
2 Replacing the pictures	Comparing textual and pictorial settings; shared writing of paragraph to describe a setting.	Demarcating sentences.	Discussing an illustrated setting in a story book; describing it in writing.	Swapping setting descriptions and choosing one piece of writing for discussion.
3 The perfect place for camping	Using a brainstorming frame to describe a landscape.		Group brainstorm followed by individual writing of first paragraph for a story; swapping texts to check spellings.	Reading and commenting on paragraphs; correcting of spellings.
4 The problem	Introducing characters to the story; suggesting ideas for story events.		Continuing their stories; checking spellings.	Choosing mis-spelled words for learning.
5 Showing the setting	Demonstrating how a setting can be shown rather than just told.	Holding a spelling test in pairs; brainstorming descriptive vocabulary.	Ending their stories.	Sharing completed stories.

Key assessment opportunities
● Test children on individual spelling lists.
● Are the children using similes and metaphors in their writing?
● Can they describe a setting by showing the scene?
● Do the children recognise the basic structure of a story?

Story settings

Objectives

NLS

T1: To compare a range of story settings, and to select words and phrases that describe scenes.
T8: To express views about a story or poem identifying specific words and phrases to support viewpoint.
S1: To use awareness of grammar to decipher new or unfamiliar words; to use these strategies in conjunction with knowledge of phonemes, word recognition, graphic knowledge and context.
W14: To infer the meaning of unknown words from context.

What you need
● Photocopiable pages 17-19
● selection of fairy stories
● the children's current stories for personal reading.

Differentiation

Less able
● Provide simple texts and assist children in selecting appropriate descriptions.

More able
● Children should select examples of similes and metaphors from their personal reading.

Shared work
● Remind the children that all stories follow the same pattern: there are always characters – in a setting – who have a problem, and the main part of most stories is about how the problem is solved.
● Stress that it is important that storytellers can create lively characters, in a vivid setting, with an interesting problem. Explain that this unit concentrates on the development of setting in story reading and writing.

Shared word- and sentence-level work
● Before distributing the texts on photocopiable pages 18 and 19, talk about the rules for working out how to read and discover the meaning of difficult vocabulary. Write a list on the board to be referred to throughout the lesson, including:

> ● Use knowledge of grammar by reading around the unknown word.
> ● Sound out letters and letter strings.
> ● Guess the meaning within the context of the known vocabulary and the sentence/story.

Guided and independent work
● Organise mixed-ability groups and appoint a good reader and a scribe for each group. Allocate *The Mousehole Cat* to half the groups and *Harriet's Hare* to the others.
● When the reader has read the passage to his/her group, the group members should discuss the questions on photocopiable page 17 for the scribe to note responses. Set a time limit of ten minutes.
● Now gather the class together and read both extracts before taking responses from each group, pointing out how clearly, but with different techniques and styles, the writers have painted the settings for these two very different stories.
● Explain that in *Harriet's Hare*, Dick King-Smith has made the setting very clear by using similes. He has told us that some things look and sound like other things so that we can imagine them even more sharply, for example, *The noises were like those heard on firework night, The field looked like a square golden blanket.* In *The Mousehole Cat*, Antonia Barber evokes the setting by telling us that the sea is a dangerous, giant cat - a metaphor. Together, identify more metaphors in the text.
● Ask for any words that the children had difficulty in reading or understanding and explore how they reached conclusions about them.
● Now ask the children to refer to the novels they are currently reading and identify and mark a short description of setting for sharing.

Plenary
● Ask the children to read a selection of chosen settings from their reading books and to talk about why they chose them. These descriptions should be displayed for reference throughout this unit.

Replacing the pictures

Objectives

NLS

T9: To generate ideas by brainstorming.

T15: To begin to organise stories into paragraphs.

S12: To demarcate the end of a sentence with a full stop and the start of a new one with a capital letter.

W5: To identify mis-spelt words in own writing.

What you need

● Story books that include well-illustrated outdoor scenes

● novels with few illustrations

● photocopiable page 17.

Shared text-level work

● Share a simple and beautifully illustrated story with the class, reading it in full if possible. Explain that the work of the authors and illustrators (or author-illustrators) combine to present a story. Often the text does not even mention the setting because the pictures present this aspect very successfully.

● In picture books for older readers, such as *The Mousehole Cat*, the author usually includes a detailed description of place and setting and the illustrator's images complement the action, characterisation and setting.

● In novels with few, if any, illustrations the author tells the complete story, including description of setting and character and the way in which these interact to generate and solve problems.

● Choose an appropriate page of a story in which the place has been shown by the illustration rather than by being described in the text. Use photocopiable page 17 to elicit ideas about the setting, reminding the children to think about what they would see, hear, smell, and feel if they were in that setting. (Write *N/A* against questions on the sheet that are not applicable to the illustration.)

● This work will develop visual, kinaesthetic and verbal learners, all of whom benefit from seeing the stimulus and from practical note-taking.

● Now organise the information to write a paragraph that could replace the picture of the setting. Go through the notes, demonstrating how to cross out unimportant detail and select main ideas.

Shared sentence-level work

● Elicit a definition for a sentence, reminding the children about demarcating the beginning of a sentence with a capital letter and the end with a full stop. Write the definition together.

Guided and independent work

● Give each group a well-illustrated story book and using the photocopiable sheet, tell the children to choose and brainstorm ideas about a picture of a setting from the book. A scribe should take contributions from every group member.

● Finally, ask the children to work individually, using group notes plus their own ideas, to write their own description of the story setting.

● Ask the children to check their own spellings and that of their group members.

● Place the texts in envelopes fixed into the back cover of the story book with the label *Texts to replace setting illustration on page X.*

Differentiation

Less able

● Less able pupils could develop a descriptive paragraph with your support.

More able

● Children should use one or two similes in their descriptive paragraph.

Plenary

● Swap books amongst the groups and ask the children to choose one piece of good writing to share with the class, with an explanation for the choice.

● Return the story books to the library, with envelopes attached, giving real purpose to the lesson.

UNIT 1 HOUR 3 Narrative: setting

The perfect place for camping

Objectives

NLS
T11: To develop the use of settings in own stories.
T12: To collect suitable words and phrases in order to write short descriptions.
T15: To begin to organise stories into paragraphs.
W5: To keep individual lists of mis-spelt words and learn how to spell them.

What you need
● Pictures of different rural or seaside settings
● large Post-it Notes.

Shared text-level work

● Tell the children that a story's setting can be so important that writers often begin their stories by establishing the setting in the opening paragraph.
● Explain that the children are going to write stories using this model, but first the class will compose an opening paragraph together.
● Divide the board into four columns, headed: *What I would see, What I would hear, What I would smell* and *What I would feel.*
● Show one of the landscapes to the children. Ask them to imagine that they are going to camp for a night in this place with a friend. Brainstorm words and phrases about the setting for each heading on the board.
● Explain that it is crucial to focus on the main points of the setting to ensure its description is not dull. Elicit which details should be deleted from the columns on the board and then ask the children to craft descriptive sentences using the remaining words and phrases.
● Remind them of using the past tense in stories and encourage the use of strong adjectives and effective adverbs.
● Tell the children that their sentences are the opening paragraph to a story about the camping trip. Ask one child to read the finished piece, emphasising that this first paragraph should make the reader want to continue reading the story.

Guided and independent work

● Divide the class into mixed-ability groups of three or four. Give each group a different picture and an A3 landscape sheet of paper divided into four columns as on the board. Ask the children to brainstorm ideas based on their picture. Either tell the children they have ten minutes to write down as many ideas as they can in each column, or give them two and a half minutes for each section.
● Then ask the children to work individually to craft their own opening paragraph, deciding on main ideas and making any important additions.
● Now ask everyone to stick a blank Post-it Note onto their work. Remind the children of the importance of correct spelling in final drafts and tell them that they will help one another with corrections. Swap the texts and ask the children to study each other's work searching for spelling errors. These should be underlined and correct spellings listed on the Post-it Notes.

Differentiation

Less able
● Give children a starter sentence: *We knew that it was the perfect place to camp...*

More able
● Children should use one or two metaphors as part of their opening paragraph.

Plenary

● Ask a few children to read out their paragraphs and encourage constructive comments on the quality of the writing.
● Display the drafts with the pictures and encourage children to read one another's work.
● Check and add to the spelling lists where appropriate.

The problem

Objectives

NLS

T15: To begin to organise stories into paragraphs.
W5: To keep individual lists of mis-spelt words and learn to spell them.
W7: To practise new spellings regularly by 'look, say, cover, write, check' strategy.

What you need

● The children's work from Hour 3
● Post-it Note spelling lists
● large Post-it Notes

Shared text-level work

● Remind the children that they have written the first paragraph for a story about a camping trip. Ask a few volunteers to read their work aloud.
● Remind the children that a story is always about characters, in a setting, who have a problem or some sort of adventure/incident. If any of these three parts are missing, there is no story.
● Tell the children that for this camping story, the setting has been introduced and that the main character is the author and one friend of the children's choice who are camping together.
● Distribute Post-it Notes and allow three minutes for children to write the heading *My characters* at the top of the Post-it Note and under this to write their own name and that of a friend who will take part in their camping adventure story.
● Write the following list of problems on the board and ask the children to choose the problem that will drive their particular story along. Say: *You wake in the middle of the night to find that*:

> ● a terrible storm has blown up
> ● the menacing silhouette of a person is seen through the canvas
> ● an enormous screeching creature is dive-bombing the tent with huge wings outspread
> ● strange snuffles and howls are sounding from the tent entrance which is *open!*

● After discussion and possibly the addition of other ideas, ask everyone to choose a problem.
● Tell the children that in the next paragraph of their story they must describe the problem and the way in which the characters try to deal with it but are unsuccessful. The paragraph should end with the characters deciding to flee.

Guided and independent work

● Ask the children to write their paragraphs and then to swap their texts with another child, to check and list spellings as in Hour 3.
● Now distribute the drafts of paragraph one. Tell the children to rewrite this paragraph, incorporating learned spellings. (As they do this, check the spelling corrections for the second paragraph.)

Differentiation

Less able
● Provide a starter sentence for paragraph two, for example, *We woke suddenly and were horrified to discover...*

More able
● Provide words of appropriate difficulty for children who do not have five spelling mistakes.

Plenary

● Tell the children to look at their spelling lists for paragraphs one and two and to choose five of the words to learn by the Look-Say-Cover-Write-Check method. Explain that there will be a test at the beginning of the next lesson and that it is every child's responsibility to learn their spellings.
● Ask the children to copy their personal lists ready for learning.

Showing the setting

Objectives

NLS
T11: To develop the use of settings in own stories.
S3: To experiment with changing simple verbs in sentences.
S5: To use the term 'verb' appropriately.
W6: To use independent spelling strategies.

What you need

● Spelling lists from previous lessons
● the children's stories so far
● a video/DVD clip showing interaction of character and setting
● Post-it Notes.

Shared word- and text-level work

● Organise the children into spelling pairs. Label them A and B and ask them to swap spelling lists. Allow three minutes for Child A to test Child B and then swap roles. Ask the children to mark their partners' papers.
● Discuss the results and ensure individuals feel responsible for their own personal development in spelling.
● Tell the children that they will now complete their camping adventure story by describing the 'flight' home. Explain that writers sometimes stand back from a setting and describe what it looks like, as in paragraph one. A different way of including setting is by showing the place through the interaction of character and setting.
● Refer to the way in which film directors create frightening scenes. They do not for example, merely present us with spooky forests with black trees and staring animal eyes. They show us how frightening a scene is through the affect the setting has on the character. For example, bent branches could clutch the character's hair and clothing, the character might cover his/her ears to block out the screeching of owls, or run in circles to escape luminous, staring animal eyes.
● Writers show the effect of setting upon character to intensify the mood, whether happy, romantic, contented or frightening.
● Tell the children that they will brainstorm ideas to help them with the final 'flight' paragraph of their story. The mood to be created is one of fear as the characters escape from the problem presented in their second paragraph.
● Divide the board in two with the headings *Adjectives/nouns* and *Adverbs/verbs*. Elicit a definition for these parts of speech and then brainstorm vocabulary. Carry the same idea across the board, possibly starting with the example above:

● Jagged, bent branches clutched painfully
● Ragged bats swooped soundlessly
● A wild cat sprang suddenly.

● Using a brainstorm of no more than five lines, demonstrate how to form action sentences with each one. For example, *As I ran, black, jagged branches clutched painfully at my clothes and hair. They seemed to pull me back!* Find as many examples as possible for each line, demonstrating that words and ideas can be changed to create different effects.

Differentiation

Less able
● Children should use the class brainstorm in writing their paragraph.

More able
● Encourage children to generate their own ideas in writing their paragraph.

Guided and independent work

● Ask the children to write the final paragraph for their stories. Explain that the story should end with the two characters bursting into one of their homes, safe at the end of a scary adventure.

Plenary

● Read and discuss some of the completed stories. Point out the way in which the setting is action-packed, rather than still.

Thinking about setting

■ Underline the place described. You may need to underline more than one.

seaside	wood	forest	mountain	farm
village	valley	park	garden	

■ Write a phrase or sentence to describe what you see:

● Colours _____

● Weather _____

● The sky _____

● Animals _____

● Plants _____

● Trees _____

● Water _____

● Beach _____

■ List three sounds that can be heard.

_____   _____   _____

■ Add any other ideas.

■ What does the character feel about what she/he is seeing in this

place? _____

_____

■ If there is a problem in this scene what is it? _____

_____

TERM 1

The Mousehole Cat

Then one year there came a terrible winter. At the far end of England the blue-green sea turned grey and black.

The Great Storm Cat is stirring, thought Mowzer as she watched at her window. The wind howled like a wild thing about the high headlands. It came hunting the fishing boats in their hidden harbours. When the Great Storm Cat is howling, thought Mowzer, it is best to stay indoors by a friendly fire.

The sea drew itself up into giant waves and flung itself against the great breakwaters. All along the coast of Cornwall, the stone walls stood the shock.

Then the sea sucked up its strength again and roared right over them, sinking the sailing boats in their home havens. But it could not get into the Mousehole.

Mowzer watched as the Great Storm Cat clawed with his giant cat's paw through the gap in the harbour wall. But it was too small.

He snarled and leaped up at the great breakwater under the lowering sky. But it was too high.

The fishing boats sat safe as mice in their own mousehole. But they could not get out.

Antonia Barber

Illustration © Nicola Bayley

Harriet's Hare

Harriet sat up, suddenly wide-awake. Whatever was that noise?

It was a rushing, tearing swishing noise-just the sound a rocket makes on Guy Fawkes Night, yet much louder. But this was the start of a midsummer day and-she looked at her watch-early too, not five o'clock yet.

She leaped out of bed and ran to the window.

The farmhouse and its buildings were tucked into the side of a gentle hill, and in the little flat valley below were two large fields, the nearer one green, the further one gold.

In the first, her father's cows would normally have been waiting around the gateway for him to come and fetch them in for morning milking. But now the whole herd was galloping and buck-jumping around the pasture as though something had scared the wits out of them.

Dick King-Smith

UNIT 2

Narrative: dialogue

For many children, the use of inverted commas is one of the easiest concepts to grasp in the complex area of punctuation. Remembering to use a capital letter within the speech marks and using some form of punctuation before closing the speech marks is more difficult. However, writing speech that sounds realistic is the main difficulty facing young writers in the area of narrative dialogue.

This unit covers punctuation conventions when recording speech and children are encouraged to listen carefully to people speaking. Developing a writer's ear for authentic dialogue is essential if children are to create rounded characters in their stories. There is also an emphasis upon the way in which the writer indicates *how* words are spoken.

The lessons demand a fast pace and offer opportunities for different learning styles. Social learning is key, with mixed-ability groups discussing, creating cartoons, checking memory and supporting one another.

Hours 4 and 5 link to Unit 2 in *Grammar for Writing*; this whole unit covers similar learning to *Grammar for Writing* Unit 4.

Hour	Shared text-level work	Shared word-/ sentence-level work	Guided and independent work	Plenary
1 Crash diet	Identifying dialogue within a short story.	Identifying dialogue and how it is indicated by speech marks.	Organising a group reading of the story; converting the story into comic strip form.	Evaluating the cartoon strips.
2 Capturing the authentic voice	Discussing the need for effective, realistic dialogue in stories.	Investigating how to present dialogue in prose.	Observing dialogue/ conversations in real life; writing in speech bubbles.	Sharing active dialogue collected and deciding which examples are the most interesting and authentic.
3 A ghastly, ghostly encounter	Reading a text with overuse of *said*; discussing improvements.	Generating synonyms for *said*; noting use of past tense.	Playing a game to generate appropriate synonyms for the text; reading new text aloud.	Building a word wall of synonyms for *said* for future reference.
4 Witness statement	Listening to, recalling and recording in writing a piece of dialogue.	Revising speech layout conventions.	Writing the heard conversation; collating an accurate group version.	Sharing written dialogues and comparing these with the actual event; discussing choice of speech tags.
5 My dog has no nose	Converting a comic strip into prose.	Revising past tense of verbs, ending in -*ed*; revising -*ing* form when used with speech.	Converting another comic strip into prose, heeding layout conventions.	Checking work against agreed criteria.

Key assessment opportunities
● Can the children transfer dialogue from prose to cartoon strip and vice-versa?
● Does each piece of dialogue begin with a capital letter and end with an appropriate piece of punctuation?
● Do the children begin a new paragraph for each new speaker?
● Do they use a variety of speech tags (other than *said*)?

Crash diet

Objectives

NLS

T2: To learn how dialogue is presented in stories.
S2: To take account of grammar and punctuation when reading aloud.
S8: To use the term 'speech marks'.

S&L

27 Group discussion and interaction: To use talk to organise roles and action.
28 Drama: To present events and characters through dialogue to engage the interest of an audience.

What you need
● Photocopiable page 26.

Shared text- and sentence-level work
● Distribute photocopiable page 26. Tell the children that the passage contains some dialogue and ask the children if they can identify it. Elicit or explain that dialogue is conversation between characters.
● Read through the text together and ask the children how we know which are the words spoken. A number of answers are acceptable here, including the use of speech tags such as *said*, but guide attention towards the speech marks. Speech marks can be described to the children as incomplete or 'corners' of speech bubbles to emphasise the fact that the words in speech marks are exactly the same as those in speech bubbles if the same story is represented in comic strip form.

Guided and independent work
● Organise the class into mixed-ability groups of three. Ask each group to appoint a narrator, another group member to read the words spoken by Alison and the other to read those spoken by Bill. Then let the children practise reading the passage. Circulate to ensure that each group is doing this correctly and with appropriate intonation and expression.
● Choose one group that has read well to perform for the rest of the class, and ask the audience for comments.
● Finally, ask each group to assess honestly their own reading of the dialogue, giving themselves marks out of five.
● Now tell the children that you want them to extract the spoken text in order to convert the passage into a cartoon strip.
● Explain that each child in the group will be responsible for illustrating and writing the speech bubbles for one frame. Allow a few minutes for the groups to designate responsibilities.
● Explain that each paragraph of the passage should correspond to one of the children's frames.
● Encourage the children to replicate the characters from the photocopiable sheet as closely as possible.
● Attach the frames in order onto backing paper with an agreed title above and the name of the cartoonists below.

Plenary
● Discuss criteria for judging each other's work, including the fact that all the text that appears in speech marks in the passage appears in speech bubbles in the comic strip.
● Ask the groups to place their work on their desks and to stand behind their chairs. Now tell them to move slowly round the class in an assessment 'carousel'. Allow the groups about thirty seconds to look at each piece of work.
● After discussion, ask each group in turn to choose their favourite comic strip and to share their decision with the rest of the class, explaining their choice.

Differentiation

Less able
● Highlight the spoken text for the children.

More able
● Encourage children to create their own cartoon strip from scratch.

UNIT 2 HOUR 2 Narrative: dialogue

Capturing the authentic voice

Shared text-level work
● This lesson requires that children observe other children in natural situations in school in order to gather authentic pieces of dialogue. This might be done by giving the class a later play time so that they can observe other children at play, or by sending them to observe and listen in the dining hall during lunch, before or after their own meal time.
● Tell the children that spoken language is different from written language. Brainstorm examples of this on the board: incomplete sentences, colloquialisms and more contractions. Explain that dialogue is useful in writing because a person's way of speaking tells us a lot about them, but authentic dialogue can be difficult to capture in writing.

Shared sentence-level work
● Remind the children of the two ways to present dialogue, giving appropriate examples, and discussing the main differences between the use of speech bubbles and speech marks:

> ● The text in speech marks is usually accompanied by a speech tag identifying the speaker, such as *said Bill*.
> ● Whenever there is a new speaker in a piece of dialogue, a new paragraph is started.

Guided and independent work
● Tell the children that they will now go on a mission to hear some interesting dialogue. Organise pairs and tell the children that each pair must write down at least two pieces of interesting dialogue. Later they will be asked to share these with the class along with an explanation of why they were chosen. Stress that interesting dialogue is often funny, but that no bad language or cheek will be accepted. Send the children into the playground or dining hall for ten minutes.
● After dialogue has been collected ask the pairs what punctuation mark should come at the end of a speech to indicate how it was spoken. Ask for questions and exclamations that have been collected and recap what the appropriate mark looks like. Speech that is neither a question nor exclamation should end with a full stop.
● Ask the pairs to transfer their rough copies of dialogue to large speech bubbles.
● Now tell the children to transfer dialogue from their speech bubbles to prose form, meeting the criteria identified in shared work.

Plenary
● Invite each pair to stick their speech bubble onto the wall, saying the words and explaining why they chose that speech.
● Conduct a class vote on the most interesting and authentically presented piece of dialogue.

Differentiation

Less able
● Emphasise that anything spoken counts as a piece of dialogue, no matter how short.

More able
● Encourage these pairs to write down exchanges between two or more children.

A ghastly, ghostly encounter

Objectives

NLS
T9: To generate ideas relevant to a topic by brainstorming, word association etc.
S4: To use verb tenses with increasing accuracy in speaking and writing.
W17: To generate synonyms for high-frequency words.
W19 To know common vocabulary for introducing and concluding dialogue.

What you need
● The children's reading books
● photocopiable page 27
● small white cards
● large coloured cards.

Shared text- and word-level work
● Begin by reading 'A ghastly, ghostly encounter' to the class. Ask the children in what way the writing could be improved. Note that the word *said* is overused.
● Ask the children if they can think of any words that could be used instead of *said* when tagging speech. Brainstorm suitable verbs in the past tense such as *whispered, shouted, asked, demanded, hissed, screamed* with the children giving examples of how each suggested word might be used.
● Following the brainstorm, ask the children to flick through their reading books to find a passage of dialogue. Tell them to skim the passage for other vocabulary for tagging dialogue. Add these words to the list and explain that words with similar meanings are called synonyms.

Shared sentence-level work
● If any notable synonyms for *said* have been missed, introduce them in the present tense and ask the children to provide the past tense, for example, *order, agree, reply*. Note the *-ed* endings of the regular verbs.

Guided and independent work
● Divide the class into groups of three and give out eight white cards to each group, along with a copy of 'A ghastly, ghostly encounter'. Ask each group to appoint a scribe and ask the scribes to write down a word from the board on each card. Tell the children to shuffle the cards and place them face down. Ask the scribe to cross out the first use of *said* in the text. One group member should turn over a card and the scribe should write this word in place of *said*. Tell the children to continue through the passage in this way until an alternative for each use of the word *said* has been found.
● Next, tell each group to appoint a reader. Ask the group to read the text together before each reader reads out their new passage using appropriate intonation, pace and volume. This can and should be very amusing!
● With reference to the passages just read out, discuss the fact that alternatives to *said* are sometimes suitable and sometimes not. Ask the groups to work together to rewrite the passage using suitable alternatives.
● As the children complete the task, assign one of the alternatives to *said* to each scribe (and other good writers as appropriate) and ask them to write the synonym in their best handwriting on a large card.

Differentiation

Less able
● Give children another copy of the passage so that they can cross out the word said when replacing it with suitable alternatives.

More able
● Encourage children to add adverbs to the speech tags to give a more powerful description of how the words are spoken.

Plenary
● Ask the children as a whole class to order the synonym cards alphabetically on the wall for use when writing dialogue in the future.
● Share some of the children's rewritten stories to note how they sound this time.

UNIT 2 HOUR 4 ▣ Narrative: dialogue

Witness statement

Objectives

NLS
T10: To write own passages of dialogue.
T15: To begin to organise stories into paragraphs
S7: To learn the basic conventions of speech punctuation.

Shared text-level work

● This lesson involves the children in transcribing real dialogue that they hear at the start of the lesson. You can arrange this in a number of ways. For example, another teacher or classroom assistant might make a remark loudly to you, or older children could come in and act out a situation. An example dialogue is given below. Whichever scenario is used, it is important that the children's attention is attracted and held, and that the script is written down in advance so that the children can compare their writing with the original. If you intend to refer to a member of staff, warn them first!

> TA: Have you heard about Mrs X?
> Teacher: What about her?
> TA: We think she must have won the lottery.
> Teacher: Oh yes? Why?
> TA: Well, she came to school today in a brand new Lamborghini.
> Teacher: You must be joking. They cost hundreds of thousands!
> TA: I know, and it's the latest model according to Billy Evans in Class F.
> Teacher: It must have been a big win then.

● Tell the children that the dialogue they have just heard was made up for the purposes of the lesson only, and that now they must try to remember what they have heard and write it down.
● Explain that recalling dialogue is what witnesses in court cases are asked to do. Challenge the children to see who would make the most reliable witnesses!
● Give the children a minute of silence, without writing anything down, to go over what they have heard.

Shared sentence-level work

● Revise the conventions of speech marks before the children begin writing, emphasising that a new paragraph must be started for each new speaker. Tell the children that they must describe the incident, getting as close as possible to the exact words that were spoken.

Guided and independent work

● Ask the children to write down their version of the incident.
● Then organise groups of four and tell the children to read their dialogues to each other. Ask them to compare their dialogues and to use them to create a group version they think is as accurate as possible. This could be done by cutting and pasting parts from their individual dialogues or by writing it out afresh.

Differentiation

Less able
● Group less able children with more able children for extra support.

More able
● Encourage children to consider the way in which the words were spoken when choosing a speech tag.

Plenary

● Ask a member from each group to read out their dialogue. Discuss the suitability of the different speech tags used. The class should vote for the version of the incident they think is most accurate before you read out the script that was used.

My dog has no nose

Objectives

NLS

T10: Using reading as a model, to write own passages of dialogue.
S4: To use verb tenses with increasing accuracy in speaking and writing.
W8: To learn how the spelling of verbs alter when ing is added.

What you need
● Photocopiable page 28
● notebooks or paper.

Shared sentence-level work
● Tell the children that they are going to be assessed on what they have learned about writing dialogue.
● Emphasise that stories are generally written in the past tense. Give the children two examples of the regular past tense – *walk* becomes *walked; shout* becomes *shouted*. Ask them how the verb changed. (-*ed* was added.) Ask for the past tense forms of *touch, point, play* and *share*. Now explain that not all verbs follow this rule. Establish the past tense forms of *see, go, eat, stand, sit, fall*.
● Give out the comic-strips and ask the children to look at the first strip. What are the words spoken in each scene? Point out that there is much more information in each scene than just the speech. What information is important enough to be included in a prose version of the comic strip? (The appearance of the characters and what they do.)

Shared word-level work
● Remind the children that one way of describing what the characters are doing while they speak is to add this information after the speech tag: *'My dog has no nose', announced Pete, putting on his shoes*. Explain that the -*ing* form of the verb is used because the action is taking place at the same time as the speech. Tell the children that there are two rules for this form of the verb:
1. If the verb ends in *e*, the *e* must be dropped before adding the -*ing*, for example, *take – taking*.
2. If the verb ends in a consonant preceded by a vowel, a double consonant must be used, for example, *run – running*.
● It may be helpful to write the -*ing* form without following the conventional rules, *takeing* and *runing*, to demonstrate how their pronunciations would be wrong.

Shared text-level work
● Convert the first comic strip to prose with the children. (Use the example on the sheet if you wish.) Recall the rules for writing dialogue taught in previous lessons.

Guided and independent work
● Ask the children to 'translate' the second comic strip into prose, reminding them of the main criteria that you will be assessing:

> ● The words spoken by a character must have speech marks around them.
> ● An appropriate speech tag must be used for each piece of dialogue.
> ● A new paragraph must be started for each new speaker.

Differentiation
● Differentiation by outcome of assessment.

Plenary
● Remind the children that this is an assessment task and ask them to check their work for one criterion at a time. Read these out, allowing a few minutes for a check of each one.

TERM 1

Crash diet

Bill was old and thin with a white beard. His wife Alison was younger, but rather overweight.

One dinner time Bill was cooking sausages. Alison came in and sat down at the table wearing a helmet.

"Why are you wearing a helmet?" asked Bill, placing the sausages on a plate.

"I'm on a crash diet" Alison replied, biting into a sausage.

A ghastly, ghostly encounter

A white shape floated towards Suki and Tom out of the darkness.

"Aaaaa—aa—aa—ggghh!" it said.

"D-dd-d-d-did y-you h-hear that?" said Suki

Putting his lips to Suki's ear, Tom said, "Suki, I think it's a ghost!"

The white shape was moving closer. Cupping her hands around her mouth to magnify the sound, Suki said, "Go away! We're not frightened of you. Shout Tom. Make a big noise. I've heard that ghosts are scared of noise!"

"Boooooh!" said Tom.

Throwing off the white sheet and giggling, Tom's sister said, "Admit it. I scared you both!"

"I don't think that was funny," said Suki, stamping her foot.

They stared angrily at each other and then suddenly, all three of them started laughing helplessly.

"Watch out though," said Tom, "We'll get you back!"

My dog has no nose

This is an example of the way in which the cartoon strip above may be rewritten as a piece of prose:

My dog has no nose

Kate was tall and thin with short brown hair. Her friend Pete was small with blonde hair. One day they were getting ready to go out.

"My dog has no nose" announced Pete, putting on his shoes.

"How does it smell?" asked Kate, opening the door.

"Terrible!" answered Pete, frowning.

Re-write the cartoon strip below as a piece of prose. You may look at the text above to remind you of how to do this.

UNIT 3

Plays

In drama it is important for children to improvise and also to interpret scripts. When writing plays, children should improvise and act before committing a script to paper. The lessons in this unit lead children through this process. The importance and purpose of punctuation is highlighted. In learning to read punctuation, children also learn how to write it as an integral part of their own playwriting.

The production and performance aspect of drama is considered in this unit, as children decide what makes a good performance. The importance of correct spelling in enabling other actors to read playscripts is stressed.

Finally, children transcribe prose to playscript. This activity provides a rigorous test of the understanding of dialogue and of the conventions of writing a play.

Hour	Shared text-level work	Shared word-/ sentence-level work	Guided and independent work	Plenary
1 The fire	Noting script layout features; reading a script aloud.	Identifying how punctuation helps understanding and interpretation in a play.	Preparing, performing and evaluating different playscript extracts.	Collating and discussing critics' comments.
2 The bully	One group create and act a play; recapping good performance criteria; evaluating the performance.		Devising, writing, performing and evaluating a play, correctly punctuated.	Identifying layout differences between a story and a play.
3 Playwrights at work	Developing criteria for a good playscript.		Developing a given scene; writing the script after rehearsal.	Discussing how it feels to be a playwright and difficulties encountered.
4 Stage directions	Revising the importance of reading the punctuation.	Revising punctuation for playscripts.	Reading, casting, rehearsing and performing a script written by another group; sharing comments with the writers.	Using new stage directions in performances.
5 A moment in time	Shared transcription of story into play.	Using speech and punctuation conventions appropriate to playscripts.	Working individually to adapt a story as a playscript.	Using agreed criteria to evaluate the scripts.

Key assessment opportunities
● How well do the children perform?
● Can they give constructive comments on others' performances?
● Can they write a playscript using appropriate conventions?
● Can children use the punctuation in a script?

UNIT 3 HOUR 1 ▢ Plays

Objectives

NLS
T4: To read, prepare and present playscripts.
T5: To recognise the key differences between prose and playscripts.
S2: To take account of the grammar and punctuation when reading aloud.

S&L
28 Drama: To present events and characters through dialogue to engage an audience.
32 Drama: To identify and discuss qualities of others' performances.

What you need
● Photocopiable pages 35 and 36
● published playscripts.

The fire

Shared text- and sentence-level work
● Distribute the 'Fire' playscript and note some of the layout features of a playscript:

> ● The scene and characters on stage are listed at the beginning.
> ● Characters names are listed in the left margin in all caps or small caps.
> ● Stage directions telling the actors what to do are written in brackets in italic. (These are not to be read aloud by the actors.)
> ● Apart from the stage directions all of the main body text is dialogue.

● Ask volunteers to read parts aloud. Afterwards, emphasise that the actors had no rehearsal time and ask the class to comment on how well the volunteers read.
● Encourage the actors to explain what features of the script told them how to read their parts.
● Explain that punctuation is central to the understanding of any piece of text. When reading a play, question marks, exclamation marks, commas and full stops dictate the manner in which words, phrases and sentences are spoken.
● Tell the children that, in groups, they will shortly be performing a play and that the audience will comment on the quality of the performance using the 'Theatre critics' help sheet'. Go through each item on the sheet with the class. Explain that any audience will be looking for these features in any play they go to see.

Guided and independent work
● Organise the class into mixed-ability groups. Ideally, each group should be issued with an extract from a different playscript (and you may wish to organise group sizes according to character numbers). If this is not possible then every group can develop their own interpretation of 'Fire'.
● Tell the children that after a short period of rehearsal time they will be performing their play for the class. Allow ten minutes reading and rehearsal time before the plays are performed.
● Organise the classroom so that each group will formally evaluate the performance of one other group using their theatre critics' sheet. Ask the children to complete their sheets independently.
● Advise the children to be positive in their written responses.

Plenary
● Collate the critics' evaluations into booklets with the name of the play and performers on the front. Booklets can then be presented to the actors, enabling them to reflect upon their performances.
● Discuss the process of performance and explain to the children that the critics' responses and advice will help them when writing and performing their own plays in the next lesson.

Differentiation

Less able
● As children rehearse in groups, give advice on punctuation to children who have difficulty in this area.

More able
● Ask children to use the evaluation booklets to write a report for the local newspaper.

The bully

Objectives

NLS
T14: To write simple playscripts based on own reading and oral work.
S2: To take account of the grammar and punctuation eg sentences, speech marks, exclamation marks and commas to mark pauses, when reading aloud.

S&L
31 Group discussion and interaction: To actively include and respond to all members of the group.
32 Drama: To identify and discuss qualities of others' performances.

What You need
● Sheets of A3 paper
● A2 backing paper
● pens
● glue.

Differentiation

Less able
● Support a group of less able children in writing their lines.

More able
● Remind children of the importance of the punctuation they use (commas, question marks, exclamation marks and full-stops).

Shared text-level work
● Tell the children that today they are going to create, dramatise and write their own drama.
● Ask for four volunteers and explain that each of them will play one of the following characters in their own play: the pickpocket, the victim, the witness, the police officer. Explain that the play should last for one minute and contain the whole story, and that each character must speak at least once.
● Send the volunteers outside the classroom to create their play. Meanwhile, remind the children of what they did in the last lesson and discuss what they will be looking for in the new performance. (A good, believable story with a satisfactory ending; lively action; audible, expressive speech, perhaps gesture and actions.)
● Invite the actors back into the classroom to begin their performance.
● Afterwards, discuss the performance using the success criteria decided by the audience. Ask the actors how they feel about the play and anything they may have added or done differently if they had more preparation time. Decide on the play's title together.

Guided and independent work
● Organise mixed-ability groups of four and tell the children that they are going to produce a play that will last for one to two minutes, called 'The bully'. Give the groups two minutes to agree on the character each person will play and a further two minutes to decide on names for their characters.
● Review the agreed success criteria and give the children a further five minutes to develop the action and dialogue before performing their plays to the rest of the class.
● Allow time for positive audience response after each performance.
● Now explain that each group is going to create a script so that their play will not be forgotten and could be performed again, by themselves or other actors.
● Ask each actor to write each of their lines of dialogue on a separate strip of A3 paper. Tell them to write their character's name at the start of each strip in block capitals, followed by a colon and then the words spoken.
● Distribute large sheets of backing paper and in their groups, ask the children to order their lines correctly on an A2 backing sheet. Tell the children to check that all the lines are in the right place before they stick them down.
● Ask each group to discuss and decide on an exciting title for their play and write this at the top of their sheet.

Plenary
● Display the playscripts and ask the children to point out the differences in layout between a playscript and a piece of prose.

UNIT 3 HOUR 3 ◼ Plays

Playwrights at work

Objectives

NLS
T4: To read, prepare and present playscripts.
T14: To write simple playscripts based on own reading and oral work
S2: To take account of the grammar and punctuation eg sentences, speech marks, exclamation marks and commas to mark pauses, when reading aloud.

S&L
28 Drama: To present events and characters through dialogue to engage an audience.

What you need
● Lined writing paper.

Shared text-level work
● Referring to the playscripts on display from Hour 2, establish differences between playscripts and prose. Write on the board *Every playscript needs...* and elicit the following:

> ● a title that makes you want to read or see the play
> ● characters' names written in capitals in a margin or column kept separate from the dialogue
> ● dialogue that reflects the way people speak in real life
> ● stage directions that help the actors to interpret their lines
> ● action and dialogue that 'tells' the story, especially if there is no narrator.

● Tell the children that they are going to write a two-minute play.
● Explain that every character must speak at least once and there should be a clear ending.

Guided and independent work
● Distribute one scenario to each group of four, such as:

> ● A bully is taking dinner money from younger children.
> ● Children have been caught writing on the toilet walls.
> ● Children find a £20 note in the playground.
> ● Children see a masked man entering a bank.
> ● A child tries to persuade friends to take a short-cut across railway tracks.
> ● Children try to stop their mother from smoking.

● Give the groups time to decide on characters and develop and rehearse the scene. They should get a clear grasp of their lines and can improvise and improve them before sitting down in a group to craft their playscripts.
● Explain that the scripts will be swapped in the next lesson and a different group will act out the plays. Therefore, clear presentation and following conventions will be imperative.
● Ask the groups to write their scripts carefully, including a title. Suggest they write on alternate lines (so that stage directions can be added later).
● Let the children perform their plays, imagining that they have never seen the script before. Ask them to correct vocabulary, punctuation and stage directions according to good performance criteria.

Differentiation

Less able
● Children should be given the task of time-keeping in the group.

More able
● Swift, legible writers should act as group scribe.

Plenary
● Discuss how it feels to be the authors of a play.

> ● Are they pleased with their plays?
> ● What was the most difficult aspect of writing the play?
> ● Are they looking forward to seeing their plays acted by another group?
> ● What problems do they envisage others having in acting out their play?

Stage directions

Objectives

NLS

T4: To read, prepare and present playscripts.
S2: To take account of grammar and punctuation, eg sentences, speech marks, exclamation marks and commas to mark pauses when reading aloud.
S10: To identify the boundaries between separate sentences in reading and in their own writing.

S&L

32 Drama: To identify and discuss qualities of others' performances.

What you need
● Playscripts developed in previous lesson
● photocopiable page 36.

Shared text-level work
● In this activity, children will use the playscripts developed in the previous lesson. Before doing this, remind them of the importance of noting punctuation in the interpretation of the lines to be spoken. Recognising that punctuation is a necessary part of the writing, affecting meaning, stress, pace and intonation, can be referred to as reading the punctuation.

Shared sentence-level work
● If necessary, revise punctuation with the children. Write the following script extract on the board, and ask the children to tell you what punctuation is missing. Elicit the use of question marks which is one of the more obvious punctuation conventions to notice. Now see if any of the lines should end with an exclamation mark and encourage the children to explain how they could tell. Ask what those sentences that are neither questions nor exclamations will end with. (A full stop.) Remind the children that all sentences begin with a capital letter. Check the children's understanding of the use of colons in playscripts, then ask if there is anywhere that a comma would help the reader to pause slightly. Ask the children to read the lines aloud before you insert the missing punctuation and capital letters.

PETE	should we wait for the crossing-patrol person
KATE	we're late I think he has already gone
PETE	do you think we should cross now
KATE	careful there's a lorry coming
PETE	we're never going to get across
KATE	stop Pete
PETE	that was close
KATE	you nearly got killed

Guided and independent work
● Tell the children that when they receive the playscript they must read it through, cast the parts and prepare a performance.
● Distribute the playscripts and allow fifteen minutes for rehearsal.
● The plays should then be performed and critiqued by the playwrights using the 'Theatre critics' help sheet'. At this point, writers should consider the differences between their expectations for how their play would be performed and the way it was actually interpreted. Ask them how their intentions could have been better described in the playscript. Having seen stage directions in the first play they acted, some pupils will recognise that these are missing or could be improved.
● Return the playscripts to the writers and ask them to insert missing stage directions or other improvements where appropriate.

Differentiation

For less able
● Children make a cover for the final playscript, including title and the names of the playwrights.

For more able
● More able children can be appointed as group leaders in what is a challenging task.

Plenary
● Redistribute the improved playscripts, enabling different groups to perform the dramas with stage directions.

A moment in time

Objectives

NLS
T5: To recognise the key differences between prose and playscripts.
T14: To write simple playscripts based on own reading and oral work.
S7: To learn the basic conventions of speech punctuation.
W5: To identify mis-spelt words in own writing.

What you need
● Photocopiable pages 37 and 38.

Shared text-level work
● Distribute photocopiable page 37 and tell the children that they are going to adapt the story as a short play.
● Recap on the differences between a playscript and a piece of prose as identified in previous lessons.
● Read the story with the children and copy the title onto the board. Now ask the children what should be written next in a playscript. (The setting and the names of the four characters.)
● Encourage the children's participation. Ask them to pick out words from the text that indicate where the story is taking place (such as *ice*, *pond*, *the wood*, *skating*, *the lane*) and craft a short description of the setting as an introductory stage direction.
● Now ask the children how they recognise the words that are spoken in a piece of narrative prose. (Those inside the speech marks.) Extract the lines of dialogue from the story and write these on the board. Add the name of the speaker in capital letters and a semi colon in front of each line of dialogue.
● Stop, or finish, the script and read through the play. Check if more dialogue is needed and discuss that if not the next step would be to insert stage directions to help actors and director/stage crew to present the action.
● Explain that in every story there is a turning point when characters make choices which dictate how the story unfolds. Tell the children that 'A moment in time' has an alternative ending and distribute the second version of the story. Read this aloud to the children and discuss the differences between the two stories.

Guided and independent work
● Explain to the children that using all the experience and knowledge they have gained in the last four lessons, you want them to work individually to convert the second story into a playscript.

Plenary
● Discuss the scripts by generating the following criteria with the children:

● Does the play have a title?
● Is there a list of characters?
● Is there a description of setting?
● Are the characters' names written down the left-hand side of the page?
● Is there a capital letter at the beginning of each piece of dialogue?
● Is there a punctuation mark at the end of every piece of dialogue?
● Are there short stage directions?
● Are the words lifted from the story correctly spelled?

● Tell the children to correct their work with reference to these criteria.

Differentiation

Less able
● Allow less able children to cut out the lines of dialogue and paste it onto backing paper, adding the characters' names.

More able
● Encourage children to include stage directions.

Fire

Mum
Ben (a 10-year-old boy)
Liam (Ben's 8-year-old brother)
Fire-fighter

(Mum, Ben and Liam are wrapped in blankets watching their house burning. The fire-fighter approaches carrying a clipboard.)

FIRE-FIGHTER: How did the fire start?

MUM: The washing machine... it somehow caught on fire and the kitchen was in flames in no time. We shut all the doors and ran out.

FIRE-FIGHTER Is everyone here who was in the house?

MUM: Yes, there were just the three of us.

BEN: Mum, where's Spider?

FIRE-FIGHTER: I wouldn't be worrying about a spider, son. You're lucky to be alive!

BEN: Spider's our dog. You said he was out, Mum, but where is he?

MUM: I'm sure he ran out in front of me.

LIAM: *(POINTING)* Oh no! There's Spider, look. There at the window.

BEN: He's trapped. We shut all the doors. Save him, please!

FIRE-FIGHTER: It's too late son.

MUM: We'll have to be brave, Ben. Nothing can be done. At least we're all safe. Where's Liam?

BEN: He's just gone round the back of the house.

MUM: Don't move from there Ben. I'll go and get him.

FIRE-FIGHTER: No, no. I'll go.

(Ben points towards the house.)

BEN: Mum! Mum! There's Liam at the window! He's in the house!

(Mum runs towards the house.)

MUM: Liam! Liam!

BEN: Break the window. Throw something through the window! Let them out!

Ben signals to Liam to get back from the window. He picks up a huge stone from the rockery and throws it through the window. Liam and Spider tumble through the billowing smoke, flames and broken glass.

LIAM: I've saved Spider.

BEN: That's good, Liam, but you could have been burned to death.

MUM: Liam, you could have been killed! Are you alright?

LIAM Yes, I'm fine. And so is Spider. Thanks, Ben, you saved our lives!

Theatre critics' help sheet

◼ You are a theatre critic. Grade each aspect of the performance on a scale of 1 to 5 with 5 being excellent.

The title of the play made you want to watch and find out more. ▢

The actors did not turn their backs to the audience. ▢

It was easy to hear the actors. ▢

The actors spoke confidently and clearly. ▢

The actors spoke with appropriate expression. ▢

The actions on the stage helped to make the story clear. ▢

There was a clear ending to the play
(The audience knew when to clap!) ▢

The play had the following message:

Do you think any parts should have been left out?

Write down one piece of advice you would offer the playwrite.

Write down one piece of advice you would offer the actors.

Signed _____ (theatre critic)

A moment in time (1)

"Are you sure the ice will hold us?" questioned Finn doubtfully. Even as he was speaking, Angus was testing the frozen surface of the pond by banging it with a long branch he had pulled over from the wood.

"It's really thick. Do you remember last year how people were skating here?" asked Angus, throwing the branch aside and beginning to prod the ice with his foot. At that moment Anne and Catherine ran down the lane to join their friends. "I wouldn't walk on that, Angus, it might break!" gasped Anne breathlessly. "Anyway, I'm freezing."

"Let's see if my mum will make us hot chocolate," suggested Catherine.

"Yeah! Come on Angus, we'll have hot chocolate and then you can ask your dad if the ice is safe to walk on," pleaded Anne.

Reluctantly, Angus turned away from the pond and joined the others walking up the lane. "Good choice, Angus," laughed Finn, slapping his younger brother on the back. "I'm sick of having to save your life!"

A moment in time (2)

"Are you sure the ice will hold us?" questioned Finn doubtfully. Even as he was speaking, Angus was testing the frozen surface of the pond by banging it with a long branch he had pulled over from the wood.

"It's really thick. Do you remember last year how people were skating here?" asked Angus, throwing the branch aside and beginning to prod the ice with his foot. At that moment Anne and Catherine ran down the lane to join their friends. "I wouldn't walk on that, Angus, it might break!" gasped Anne breathlessly. But Angus had already walked several steps from the side and was starting to slide around on the shiny surface.

"Oh, great! I'm coming too!" laughed Catherine, pretending to skate as she followed Angus.

"Come on you lot," yelled Angus, turning round and round with his arms outstretched and his face looking up to the blue sky.

"It's brilliant," laughed Catherine.

With a terrifying crack, the ice broke beneath Angus' feet and he disappeared into the black water. Catherine fell over, but the ice held precariously beneath her.

"Here, take this!" yelled Finn, desperately pushing the branch towards Catherine.

"Help me," pleaded Angus as he rose from the dark water and clutched desperately at the ice which broke beneath his grasp.

"The branch! The branch! Catherine, take the branch!" Lying on his stomach, Finn pushed the branch towards Catherine.

"I'm going for help," cried Anne as she disappeared up the lane.

As Angus surfaced a second time from the icy depths of the pond Catherine and Finn were yelling together.

"Grab this, Angus! Grab the branch!"

Finn was snaking over the ice on his stomach towards Catherine, and as Angus lunged for the branch with the last of his strength, Finn's strong hands grabbed the other end, helping Catherine to take the weight of the desperate boy.

"Stay down, Catherine. Move backwards carefully. Don't let go, Angus," ordered Finn sharply.

"Your dad's on his way," shouted Anne from the bank. "You're almost back on land," she encouraged her friends through tears. "You're going to be OK, Angus," she cried.

As the three exhausted children lay shivering on the frozen grass, Angus reached out a trembling hand, blue with cold and grasped Finn's arm. "Thanks, brother" he said. "You saved my life."

UNIT 4

Poetry

This unit begins with a celebration, a big read and a sharing of favourite poetry. The idea of a community of poets is introduced and children are given anthologies which will be central to the development of critical thinking about poetry. From the first lesson there is an emphasis upon the analysis of poetry and the expectation that children articulate their opinions. Lesson six is a dynamic introduction to writing a class composition through drama. The critical importance of figures of speech, word choice, grammar and punctuation are examined in the closing lessons.

The organisation of a poetry celebration at the end of the unit could include a choral poetry performance or the dramatic re-enactment of a playground poem for an audience of parents. Parents could also share their own favourite poems with the children. A record of critical thinking about poetry and examples of children's writing could build into a gallery of creativity to be viewed by visitors.

Hours 4 and 5 link to Unit 3 in *Grammar for Writing.*

Hour	Shared text-level work	Shared word-/ sentence-level work	Guided and independent work	Plenary
1 I like it because...	Reading and discussing 'Listen', giving reasons for preferences.	Using punctuation as a guide to reading a poem.	Choosing and reading a poem; explaining their choice; commenting on readings.	Naming a poem they have heard and liked and saying why they like it.
2 An anthology to be proud of	Sharing chosen poetry within genres; generating criteria for a good poetry anthology.		Copying their chosen poems to begin personal anthologies.	Viewing poems and commenting on presentation.
3 Unlocking meaning	Critical study of 'For Mugs'; annotating for meaning.		Group study of a poem with the help of an investigation sheet.	Discussing poem responses; adding 'For Mugs' to anthologies.
4 Performing and understanding poetry	Reading two poems on similar theme.		Group study of the poem, using the investigation sheet.	Comparing the two poems; choosing one for anthologies.
5 Sounds great!	Working out how to read a poem that consists only of phonic sounds.	Using phonics and punctuation to help guide understanding of nonsense poems.	Group study and interpretation of two lines followed by a class choral recitation; studying new poems, identifying real and false words; writing group 'firework' poems.	Sharing 'firework' poems and adding poems to anthologies.

UNIT 4 ◼ POETRY

Hour	Shared text-level work	Shared word-/ sentence-level work	Guided reading/ writing	Independent work	Plenary
6 Playground explosion!	Re-enacting playground sounds to develop into a poem.		Writing poem lines on strips of paper arranged in a star burst on the wall; using ideas from the wall to write playground poems.	Reading the sound-burst poem followed by comments; sharing individual poems; continuing anthologies.	Matching word cards to words on the board. Identifying sounds with various spellings.
7 Poets' tricks	Reading 'Charlotte's Dog', noting descriptive words and phrases, assessing the 'truth' of the poem.	Modelling how to compile a glossary for anthologies.	Choosing favourite similes and metaphors used in the poem; adding poem to anthologies.	Sharing choices and explanations.	Sharing couplets. Focusing on long-vowel digraphs and rhymes.
8 Guess the person	Re-reading 'Charlotte's Dog', playing a metaphor game.	Revising spellchecking strategies.	Group metaphor poem, followed by individual composition, based upon group effort; continuing anthologies.	Working out who the famous person is as described by metaphors.	Reading and discussing new verses, focusing on rhyme.
9 Painting with words	Collecting words for a poem inspired by a vista, linking them to make lines of the poem.	Brainstorming synonyms for some of the suggested words; using a thesaurus.	Using a poetry frame to write 'word-picture' poems; continuing anthology collection.	Sharing rough drafts and finalised poems, examining improvements.	Discussing different uses of capital letters.
10 Kenning	Reading 'Black Dot' and examining its layout and use of kennings; brainstorming kennings for another creature.	Improving verb choices; using a thesaurus.	Writing their own list-style kennings poem; reorganising/rewriting certain lines; adding to anthology.	Sharing the poems and working out the animals described.	Sharing poems, focusing on spelling and discussing how punctuation affects reading.

Key assessment opportunities
● Can the children recite a poem with expression, using punctuation to help with interpretation?
● Can they write a list poem describing a scene?
● Can they analyse and discuss poetry?
● Do they understand the use of metaphors and similes, onomatopoeia and alliteration?

I like it because...

Objectives

NLS
T6: To read aloud and recite poems.
T8: To express their views about a poem
S2: To take account of the grammar and punctuation when reading aloud.

S&L
29 Speaking: To choose and prepare poems for performance.

What you need

- Photocopiable page 51
- range of poetry anthologies.

Shared text- and sentence-level work

- Tell the children that over the next few weeks they will be forming a community of poets. They will read and study poetry together and alone; they will become poets; they will compile an individual anthology of poetry, and finally, at the end of the unit, they will enjoy a celebration of poetry.
- Explain that they are going to choose and share a poem but that you will first share a favourite poem with them. Display and read 'Listen', using the punctuation to guide your reading. Demonstrate that you do not pause at the end of a line unless a comma, full stop or colon indicates that you should.
- Discuss your interpretation of the poem and give two reasons why you like it, perhaps because:

  - the poem has helped you to listen more carefully
  - the image of the mist is easy to picture
  - you like the idea of stars clicking on, as though by light switches
  - you like the soft sounds used by the poet.

- Explain that it is important when choosing and sharing poems to express the reasons for our preferences.
- Next, ask the children for their responses to the poem. Encourage use of a format such as *I like it/do not like it because...*
- Remind the children about the use of punctuation in guiding the reader and afterwards re-read the poem together.

Guided and independent work

- Distribute a variety of poetry anthologies among mixed-ability groups of four or five. Tell the children to choose a short poem each to read to their group.
- Allow a further ten minutes for quiet reading aloud and rehearsal, emphasising the importance of expressive reading and taking note of punctuation. Remind the children that absence of punctuation marks at the end of a line indicates that two or even three lines may have to be read in one breath.
- Taking turns, ask the children to read their chosen poem to the group, giving one reason for their choice of poem.
- After the readings each child in the group should comment on other people's choices, using the formula *I like/don't like it because...*

Differentiation

Less able
- Help children in articulating reasons for choices and in practising reading the poem.

More able
- Ask children to record their favourite poetry onto CD or cassette to be shared with parents and used as a benchmark for their performances.

Plenary

- Ask the children to name a poem they have heard and liked today and to explain why they enjoyed it. They should not choose their own poem. Some clear favourites will emerge and these should be performed by the children who chose them.
- Ask the audience to comment on the performances in terms of expression, clarity and pace.

An anthology to be proud of

Objectives

NLS
T7: To distinguish between rhyming and non-rhyming poetry and comment on the impact of layout.
W21: To ensure consistency in size and proportions of letter and the spacing between letters and words.

What you need
- Photocopiable page 51
- booklets for anthologies
- poems chosen in Hour 1
- large Post-it Notes.

Shared text-level work
- Ask the children to have their chosen poem ready for reading. Recap ways of reading punctuation, which helps to give meaning to poetry. Allow two minutes for reading the poems quietly.
- Next, ask volunteers to read a chosen poem from each of the following categories:

  - a funny or amazing poem
  - a sad poem
  - a rhyming poem
  - a non-rhyming poem.

- Ask the children to explain why they chose their poems, and encourage responses from the audience.
- It is likely that the only poem that does not rhyme is 'Listen'. Remind the children that poetry does not have to rhyme. Discuss the different forms and styles of poetry shared from the anthologies.
- Distribute blank anthology booklets and explain to the children that they are going to create their own collection of poems. Today they will copy their chosen poem, along with the explanation for why it was chosen. Discuss the way in which the poems should be displayed on their pages. List some desirable qualities on the board, taking ideas from the anthologies. For example:

  - Every page is carefully designed.
  - Writing must be legible and attractive.
  - Lines must be correctly spelled and punctuated.
  - The page may be decorated and illustrated.
  - There must be a title and the name of the poet.

Guided and independent work
- Remind the children of the importance of consistency in size and proportion of letters and spacing between letters and words when writing. Relate this to the published texts they have examined.
- Now ask the children to create their pages for the anthology, decorated, with illustrations, borders or illuminated first letters as required. Remind them to add their reasons for choosing the poem.
- Leave a few blank pages at the beginning of the booklets as these will eventually be contents and dedication pages.
- Distribute Post-it Notes and ask everyone to attach their name to the page on which they have written their poem.

Differentiation

Less able
- Assist children in decisions about page layout and presentation.

More able
- Encourage children to choose more challenging poetry.

Plenary
- Arrange open anthologies on desks or cupboard tops around the edge of the classroom. Tell the children to slowly move around the anthologies in a 'carousel', to view everyone's work. Explain that they are not expected to read the poems, but to form a quick impression of the beauty of each first page. Every child should choose at least one person who has done a good job and be able to explain why.

Unlocking meaning

Objectives

NLS

T8: To express their views about a poem, identifying specific words and phrases to support their viewpoint.

S&L

26 Listening: To follow up others' points and show whether they agree or disagree in a whole-class discussion.
31 Group discussion and interaction: To actively include and respond to all members of the group.

What you need
● Photocopiable pages 52 and 53
● anthology presentation criteria agreed in Hour 2.

Shared text-level work
● Explain to the children that often in poetry every word carries a strong meaning. Poets cut out unnecessary words and leave only those that are powerful in communicating their message.
● Display and read the poem 'For Mugs'.
● Explain that you are going to annotate around the poem and that this is a very useful way of studying poetry.
● Having read the poem a second time, ask the children to say in a sentence what they think the poem is about. Write the general meaning at the top of the poem: *This is about a dog that has died.*
● Ask the children if the poem rhymes and elicit the rhyming pattern. Join rhymes with a curved line.
● Ask which lines project a picture in the mind and ask for favourite images. Annotate these on the text. Encourage the children to give you examples of words and phrases that show how sad the poet is, and annotate the poem with these responses.

Guided and independent work
● Distribute photocopiable page 53 and organise a scribe for each group who will annotate the group copy of the poem.
● Tell the children to read the poem first and then discuss each question in the poetry investigation in turn. Allow fifteen minutes for this discussion/study time. This collaborative approach to unlocking the meaning of poetry is favoured by social learners. It is important that non-social learners are encouraged to work in this way, perhaps by appointing them as chair or scribe or speaker.

Plenary
● Gather the children together for a class discussion of responses.
● Before starting the discussion, lay down clear rules, for example:

● Indicate you want to speak by raising your hand.
● Do not interrupt the speaker.
● Listen carefully so that points are not repeated.
● Every point of view is valid, but no 'put-downs'!

Differentiation

Less able
● Children could work in a group with you. Alternatively, move amongst the groups, to ensure these children are included.

More able
● Children should act as chairmen, encouraging others to contribute before offering their own interpretation.

● Allow each group, in turn, the opportunity to lead with their answers. Follow this with a general sharing of ideas.
● Keep the interest level high by asking for general responses where appropriate, for example, *Put up your hand if you agree/disagree with this, and be ready to explain why.*
● When groups ask questions about aspects of the poem they did not understand, try to coax answers from those or other children before giving your own response.
● Finally, ask the children to copy the poem into their anthologies.
● Remind them of the criteria for design and presentation.

Performing and understanding poetry

Objectives

NLS
T6: To read aloud and recite poems, comparing different views of the same subject; to discuss choice of words and phrases and create impact.
T8: To express their views about a poem, identifying words and phrases to support their viewpoint.
S6: To secure knowledge of question marks and exclamation marks in reading, understanding their purpose.

What you need
● Photocopiable pages 53-55
● personal anthologies.

Shared text-level work
● Remind the children that in Hour 3 they read a sad poem about the death of a beloved dog. Today they are going to read two very different poems about two very different dogs. Display and read 'Old Boy', being careful to read the rhythm and the alliteration in, for example, *plods so ponderously*.
● Ask the children to read the poem aloud, but do not discuss meaning at this stage.
● Follow the same process for 'Heads or Tails?'. Ask why some words are written in italic. (The italic helps to establish rhythm and emphasis.)
● Split the class into four groups, with each group reading one verse. Then ask the groups to change verses.

Guided and independent work
● Organise mixed-ability groups, appoint scribes and distribute 'Old Boy' to half the class and 'Heads or Tails?' to the other half. Ask the groups to study and annotate their poem with the help of the investigation sheet. This work favours verbal/symbolic learners who enjoy responding to prompt questions and studying the structures of other people's writing. Social learners also respond well to this type of collaborative task.

Plenary
● Gather the class together and make sure that everyone has sight of both poems. Consider each question on photocopiable page 53 in relation to both poems, so that the stark contrast between forms and meanings is obvious. (The process of enquiry should be conducted as in Hour 3.) Main contrasts that will emerge from discussion are likely to be:

● The first poem is sad, as demonstrated by words like, *Bleary-eyed, stiff, wheezing, A bygone memory*. The second poem is funny as shown by phrases like *Nobody knows if it's in reverse, The darned thing's dead... it's upside down!* There is also a proliferation of exclamation marks.
● The melancholy in the first poem is emphasised by the measured pace, slowed by the short lines. The jaunty pace of the second poem is established by rhyme and rhythm. Snatches of dialogue also maintain the pace.
● Both poems paint very clear pictures. The first image unfolds slowly, the second is like a cartoon, spilling over with overlapping images.
● The first dog, although old, remains serious and stately and has clearly been a grand animal. The second dog will never be taken seriously and is a real mongrel.
● It will be interesting to discuss whether or not Kit Wright intends us to believe that the dog really is *horrible* and *hideous*.

● Finally, ask children to copy their favourite of the two poems into their anthologies.

Differentiation

Less able
● Study 'Heads or Tails?', enabling children to contribute during class discussion.

More able
● Early finishers should annotate one of the poems for the wall using additional ideas gained in discussion.

44

Sounds great!

Objectives

NLS
T12: To collect suitable words and phrases, in order to write poems; design simple patterns with words, use repetitive phrases; write imaginative comparisons.
S6: To secure knowledge of question marks and exclamation marks in reading, understanding their purpose.
W6: To sound out using phonemes; use visual skills.
W14: To infer the meaning of unknown words from context.

S&L
29 Speaking: To prepare poems for performance.

What you need
● Photocopiable pages 56 and 57.

Shared text-level work
● Tell the children that one reason why poetry is so interesting is that poets make their own rules for how poetry should be written. Display 'The Loch Ness Monster's Song'. Check that children know the legend of the monster.
● Enjoy the fact that this poem is not written using recognisable words. Children will have to call upon their knowledge of phonics in order to sound out the syllables and work out the monster's language!
● Remind the children of how they decode words as they read by sounding letters and groups of letters together. The children can also search for common strings of letters.

Shared word- and sentence-level work
● Discuss the punctuation marks in the poem and elicit what each of them tells us about how the line must be read. (Are they able to read the questions without the typical signifier question words?)
● Say some of the lines by using a pointer to indicate each group of phonics and familiar letter strings as the children 'translate' the text into sounds. Have individuals read some of the lines with the rest of the class agreeing or disagreeing with interpretations.

Guided and independent work
● Organise the class into six groups and give two lines of the poem to each group with one taking the last four short lines. Allow three minutes of rehearsal time before holding a class recital. Swap some of the lines around to maximise fun interpretation of this dynamic poem.
● Now ask the children to read 'The Ghost House' silently.
● Share lines between groups and allow three minutes of practice before giving a class recital. Check that all of the children understand the surprise.
● Ask if any of the words are invented words like those in the previous poem. Ask the groups to divide a piece of paper in two and write real words from the poem on one half and invented words on the other.
● Now, in groups of four, ask the children to take 'fireworks' as a theme and list real and invented words to represent the sounds of fireworks going off. Ask the children to use the group brainstorm to write individual sound poems entitled 'Fireworks'. They may choose to model the poem on 'The Loch Ness Monster's Song' and use only invented sounds, or they may choose to write one line describing colours and shapes and make alternate lines a list of sounds.

Plenary
● Share some of the poetry before asking the children to write and illustrate them in their anthologies.
● The two sound poems studied in class may be used in the recital for Poetry Day.

Differentiation

Less able
● Support children in writing down phonically the words they invent.

More able
● Discuss onomatopoeia and ask children to list onomatopoeic words in the poems studied.

Playground explosion!

Objectives

NLS

T9: To generate ideas relevant to a topic by brainstorming, word association etc.

T12: To collect suitable words and phrases, in order to write poems; design simple patterns with words.

T13: To invent calligrams and a range of shape poems, selecting appropriate words and careful presentation. Build up class collections.

What you need

● Long, narrow strips of A3 paper.

Differentiation

Less able

● Encourage children to invent a line of poetry orally, but support them in translating this into correctly spelled and punctuated writing.

More able

● Using playground chalk, early finishers should copy their poems onto the playground.

Shared text-level work

● Remind the children of poetic sound effects and onomatopoeia they have looked at and tell them that they are going to compose a dramatic sound poem on the theme of 'Our playground'.

● Explain that before writing they will perform a dramatic re-enactment of the playground scene. Ask the children to imagine wandering around the playground hearing snippets of conversation, the sounds as people play football or tag, chants and so on. Note these on the board.

● Clear a space for all the children to lie comfortably in a circle with their feet at the centre. Tell the children to close their eyes and imagine they are in the playground.

● Remind them of how only a few children leave the building at first, building up to a crescendo which stops at the final whistle and slowly dies down to silence. Ask them to think of the sounds and words they will use in re-enacting playtime.

● Blow the whistle to start and end the drama. When you are satisfied with their performance, tell the children to break the circle and sit down. This approach to composing poetry favours kinaesthetic, active learners.

Guided and independent work

● Distribute strips of A3 paper. Remind the children of the 'Loch Ness Monster' and 'Ghost House' poems. Ask the children to write one line for the playground poem, showing some of the words, phrases and non-word sounds they contributed to the oral sound poem. Remind them of the importance of punctuation in enabling readers to interpret the poem. Were their words: questions, exclamations or ordinary conversations?

● Ask the children to swap their lines with a partner to check that another person is able to interpret the words correctly. Necessary changes should be made, then the strips should be assembled on a large sheet of paper with the lines radiating out from the centre in a burst of sound.

● Finally ask the children to write individual short poems, this time demonstrating the build up of sound, climax of noise and silence after the final whistle.

● Encourage children to experiment with form, possibly using a version of the radiating strip idea, or simply writing a list poem.

Plenary

● Read the class sound-burst poem. Does it matter which line starts the poem?

● Listen to a range of playground sound poems, inviting pupils to comment.

● Poems should be stuck or re-written into anthologies.

● The group drama should be re-enacted as part of the poetry celebration day.

Poets' tricks

Objectives
T6: To discuss choice of words and phrases that describe and create impact.
T8: To express their views about a poem, identifying specific words and phrases to support their viewpoint.
W13: To collect new words from reading and create ways of categorising and logging them, eg personal dictionaries, glossaries.

What you need
● Photocopiable page 58
● personal anthologies.

Shared text- and word-level work

● Display and read 'Charlotte's Dog'. Explain any unfamiliar vocabulary. The most difficult word will probably be *plimsolls*. In most areas of the country now these would probably be called trainers or gym shoes.
● Explain that some poetry anthologies provide a glossary, and discuss what information a glossary provides.
● Tell the children that in their anthologies they will put glossary words at the foot of the poem, identified with an asterisk.
● Demonstrate this for *plimsoll* and tell the children that when they include 'Charlotte's Dog' in their anthologies, they should also include the definition for this word.
● Explain that, from now on, the development of a glossary should be a part of the anthology work, with vocabulary decided as a class or individuals, as appropriate.
● Ask the children to comment on the appearance of Charlotte's dog. Discuss all the features described: ears, teeth, coat, nose, tail and eyes. Focus on the poet's method of helping our understanding by likening the dog to other images that readily spring to mind, such as *teeth like prongs of electric plugs*. What does *squashed ball bounced in the rain* tell us about the dog's nose? Explain that these images are called 'similes'. Compare them with a metaphor like *His back's a thundery winter's sky, Black clouds, white clouds rumbling by* where one thing is another. What does this metaphor tells us about the dog's coat?
● Ask the children if the poet has used a simile or a metaphor to describe the dog's tail (metaphor). Discuss the impact of the metaphor.

Guided and independent work

● Ask the children to work in groups to examine the sounds made by Charlotte's dog in verses 5 and 6. Tell them to take each sound in turn and decide if it is described by a simile or a metaphor and to comment on how effectively these figures of speech have summed up the essence of the dog. Identify and organise an able child to scribe for each group and annotate the poem with the responses.
● Allow five minutes or so for this activity and then ask the children to copy the poem into their anthologies, underlining their favourite powerful simile and favourite powerful metaphor. Next to the underlining the children should write: *This is my favourite simile/ metaphor because...*

Plenary

● Share some of the groups' annotated responses, ensuring that the less able group contribute.
● Ask a few children to read out their choice of best simile/metaphor and to show their glossary addition(s).

Differentiation

Less able
● Give direct teaching of the guided activity.

More able
● Good writers should scribe for groups in annotating the poems.

Guess the person

Objectives
T9: To generate ideas relevant to a topic by brainstorming, word association, etc.
W5: To identify mis-spelt words in own writing.
W6: To use independent spelling strategies.

What you need
● Photocopiable page 58
● personal anthologies.

Shared text-level work

● Re-read 'Charlotte's Dog'. Share some favourite similes and metaphors from the previous lesson. Revise that a simile describes one thing looking or sounding *like* another, whilst a metaphor says that one thing actually *is* another thing conveying the very essence of its being.

● Play a metaphor game. Write a heading such as piece of furniture on the board and ask the children to say what piece of furniture best summarises their character and personality. Play the game using a range of headings: article of clothing, type of food, holiday destination, type of weather.

● Tell the children that as a class they are going to construct a metaphor poem about someone they know. Decide upon a famous person together and then through discussion choose what sort of food best sums up this person. For example, a favourite actress may be described as *A warm golden pot of honey*. The second line of the poem should describe the person as, for instance, a piece of furniture: *A tall thin coat stand*. Subsequent lines could be a garment of clothing, type of weather, an animal, a place in the world (*She is a warm beach* or *the top of an icy mountain*).

Shared word-level work

● Remind the children of the importance of correct spelling. Elicit ways of checking for errors and write ideas on a large sheet of paper to be displayed as a reminder. The list should include:

● Underline a word that may be incorrect.
● Does the word look correct (shape, length and so on)?
● When sounded out, does the word sound correct?
● Does the word rhyme with other words that may use the same letter strings/ patterns?
● If still unsure check in a dictionary.

Guided and independent work

● Ask the children to decide in groups on a famous person or a person known to the whole class. They should work upon metaphors derived from the list used in shared work and possibly adding or substituting ideas such as an ornament, a type of car, a piece of music, a drink. Allow fifteen minutes for discussion and writing.

● Next, ask the children to work individually to reorganise, change and add ideas to compose a personal metaphor poem.

● Before they copy their poems into the anthologies, ask the children to check spellings.

Plenary

● Share individual poems, emphasising the fact that choice of metaphors, if apt, should lead to the class being able to identify the person in the poem.

Differentiation

Less able
● Work with children to produce a group poem for the anthologies.

More able
● Children should decide different or additional categories for metaphors and add them to their poems.

Painting with words

Objectives
T9: To generate ideas relevant to a topic by brainstorming, word association etc.
T12: To collect suitable words and phrases, in order to write poems.
W16: To understand the purpose and organisation of the thesaurus, and to make use of it to find synonyms.
W17: To generate synonyms for high-frequency words.

What you need
● Photocopiable page 59
● thesauruses
● in the absence of views from the windows, pictures of interesting scenes
● personal anthologies.

Shared text- and sentence-level work
● Tell the children that they are going to compose a word painting together, describing either a picture or a view from a window. Explain that the final poem must capture the essence of the view, enabling readers to imagine the important aspects of the scene as exactly as possible.
● First, decide on the five most important nouns or 'things' that can be seen. Write all contributions down the middle of the board, then through class debate trim the list to the required five.
● Next, ask the children to search for exactly the right adjectives to describe each noun. It will be necessary to brainstorm synonyms to find just the right word. Write selected adjectives in front of the nouns and trim these to one or two through discussion.
● Each line should now be completed with a verb or 'doing' phrase, describing what the noun is doing in the scene, for example, *Sun shining brightly in the morning sky* or *Sun glowing softly through the morning mist*. Consider a number of phrases and discuss alternatives to find the best verb to carry the line forward.
● Complete the poem by composing a final line that summarises the overall scene.

Shared word-level work
● The final version of the poem will emerge from a mass of crossing out, arrows and asterisks! Read it to the children and remind them of how crucial precision is in the limited space of a poem.
● Explain that a thesaurus can be helpful in pursuing the right word. Demonstrate how words are organised in this writers' tool. Try altering weak vocabulary in the class poem by searching for synonyms in the thesaurus.

Guided and independent work
● In mixed-ability groups, ask the children to compose word-painting poems using photocopiable page 59 and a thesaurus.
● Revise methodology with reference to the class poem and point out that there is room on the sheet for lots of revision of ideas and vocabulary. The stimulus for this poem may be an alternaive picture or a view from a different window.
● Allow fifteen minutes for the group poem to be composed and after this, ask the children to reorganise and personalise the group ideas to produce their own poem for their anthologies.

Differentiation
Less able
● Children should produce a list poem composed of adjectives and nouns only.

More able
● Emphasise the importance of the most effective adverb to describe the verb.

Plenary
● Share some of the group poems. Examine rough copies, emphasising the fact that good final drafts will only result from a great deal of brainstorming, reference to thesauruses and editing.
● Then look at some of the individual poems from those groups and discuss interesting changes and improvements.

UNIT 4 HOUR 10 Poetry

Kenning

Shared text- and word-level work

- Display 'Black Dot' and examine the layout first – a long, thin shape with very few words.
- Then read the poem to the children. Note the rhyming couplets and elicit that it is a list of physical changes, characteristics and actions that summarises the essence of a frog. Look at verses three to five in which the poet has used typical frog actions to convey in few words exactly what a frog is like.
- Tell the children that they are going to use the same technique to describe another animal, for example, a lion. Brainstorm suitable verbs, such as roar, stalk, pounce, race, sleep, bound, stare, blink.
- Explain that we can change these verbs to nouns by adding the suffix *er*: roarer, stalker, pouncer, racer, sleeper... to list what the animal is in essence, rather than just what it does.
- To improve upon this, work to find the most apt adjective to describe each noun. The thesaurus could also be used here. The list will read something like: bellowing roarer, stealthy stalker, lightening pouncer, swift racer, all day sleeper, powerful bounder, terrifying starer. (The poem does not have to rhyme.)
- When seeking the best adjective, point out that alliteration can be a powerful tool in improving the dynamic sound and meaning of a line. At this stage, it is sufficient for children to be told that alliteration is a figure of speech when the same letter or sound is used to begin several words in a row, as in the poem: *cool kicker, sitting slicker, panting puffer.*
- In order to reach a final version of the poem, lines may be reorganised according to the children's preferences.

Guided and independent work

- Ask mixed-ability groups to take the same steps in writing a list poem about an animal of their choice. Recap the steps to be taken and write them on the board, for example:

- Decide upon an animal.
- Write a list of verbs summarising animal's main actions/sounds
- Change these verbs into nouns by adding the suffix *er*.
- Add a carefully thought-out adjective that precisely describes the noun.
- Reorganise the lines to compose a poem.

- Also suggest that they do not include the name of the animal; rather end the poem with the line *Who am I?*.
- Individuals should then copy their group poem into their individual anthologies with the names of all group poets signed below.

Plenary

- Share the poems with the class. Ask the children to work out which animal is being described, and call for critical comment upon vocabulary choices and powerful images. Ask the children, with a show of hands, to choose their favourite poem.

Listen

Silence is when you can hear things.

Listen:

The breathing of bees,

A moth's footfall,

Or the mist easing its way

Across the field,

The light shifting at dawn

Or the stars clicking into place

At evening.

John Cotton

*Conversational style
Initial statement is
followed by a single-word
line, an instruction*

*List of metaphorical
descriptions; imaginative
use of vocabulary to evoke
pictures and sense of
atmosphere*

For Mugs

He is gone now. He is dead.

There is a hurting in my head.

I listen for his bark, his whine.

The silence answers. He was mine.

I taught him all the greatest tricks.

I had a way of throwing sticks

So he could catch them, and a ball

We bounced against the backyard wall.

I can see him, chasing cats,

Killing all the mountain rats,

Drinking water from his bowl.

There's a place he had a hole

To bury bones, but now it's gone.

His footprints fade upon the lawn.

He used to snuggle on my bed

But now he's gone. He died. He's dead.

Myra Cohn Livingston

Subject is immediately stated – the death of someone very significant and the effect on the author

Short sentences establishing the finality of what has happened and its effect.

Rhyming couplets (the first two are self-contained)

[VERSE 3] Style becomes more expansive and conversational

[VERSE 7 LINE 2] What effect does this line have? Why is this a more poetic image?

[VERSE 8] Return to reflections of emotion then...

[LAST VERSE] ...No-nonsense reality

Poetry investigation

1. What is the poem about – in one sentence?

_____

2. Is this a sad or happy poem? Why?

_____

3. What does it make you think of?

_____

4. Which is your favourite line, and why?

_____

5. Which is your favourite verse, and why?

_____

6. Does any part of the poem project pictures in your mind?

_____

7. Are there any words or phrases particularly good for reading aloud?

_____

8. Where the poem rhymes, link the rhyming words with a curved line.

_____

9. Write down two words/phrases that you do not understand.

_____

10. Think of an alternative title.

_____

11. Have you read another poem by this poet? If so, what was it called?

_____

12. Write one question you have about the poem.

_____

13. Note one question that the poem makes you ask about the world.

_____

Old Boy

I don't see him now
As I once did.
Bleary eyed, and sagging jowls,
Stiff of gait
And slow of step.
With a wheezing breath
He plods so ponderously
On a creaking porch.
A bygone memory
Of his fierce youth.
Just like his owner.

Neela Mann

Sadness at the passage from vitality to decay

Alliteration
[wheezing] Onomatopoeia
[creaking] Appropriate to dog too

[fierce] Contrast
[last line] Personal touch

Heads or Tails?

Dave Dirt's dog is a horrible hound,
  A hideous sight to see.
When Dave first brought it home from the pound,
We couldn't be certain which way round
  The thing was supposed to be!

Somebody said, 'If that's its *head*,
  It's *far* the ugliest dog in town.'
Somebody said, 'The darned thing's *dead*!'
  'Don't be silly, it's *upside-down*!'
'It's *inside out*!' 'It's a sort of *plant*!'
'It's wearing *clothes*!' 'It's Dave Dirt's *aunt*!'
  'It's a sort of *dressing-gown*!'

Each expert had his own idea
  Of what it was meant to be
But everybody was far from clear-
  And yet . . . we *did* agree
That Dave Dirt's dog was a horrible hound
  And a hideous sight to see!

It *loves Dave Dirt*. It follows him round
  Through rain and sun and snow.
When set in motion, it looks far *worse*,
And nobody knows if it's in reverse
  Or the way it's supposed to go!

Kit Wright

Contrasts with 'Old Hound'

Each verse is self-contained, with its own rhythm and rhyme scheme

Ideas are amusing and accessible

Rhythm is fairly regular in each verse and the conversational tone makes it ideal for recitation

Storyline – where did Dave get the dog?

Does Dave's other name suggest anything about him?

What sort of relationship do they have?

The Loch Ness Monster's Song

Sssnnnwhufffffll?
Hnwhuffl hhnnwfl hnfl hfl?
Gdroblboblhobngbl gbl gl g g g g glbgl.
Drublhaflablhaflubhafgabhaflhafl fl fl-
gm grawwwww grf grawf awfgm graw gm.
Hovoplodok-doplodovok-plovodokot-doplodokosh?
Splgraw fok fok splgrafhatchgabrlgabrl fok splfok!
Zgra kra gka fok!
Grof grawff gahf?
Gombl mbl bl-
blm plm,
blm plm,
blm plm,
blp.

Edwin Morgan

A literary joke!
Lots of fun to recite
Plenty of phonics revision!
Some strings of letters that are unusual for us in that they omit vowels
The poem demonstrates the importance of punctuation in interpretation of the texts!

The Ghost House

Don't go near the Ghost House. Don't go near!
Don't go near the Ghost House or you will hear:

Rhyme in couplets; then alternate rhymes

The flutter of bats
Flitter flutter flitter flutter
The scratching of rats
Scritch scratch scritch scratch.

Strong rhythm

Don't go near the Ghost House. Don't go near!
Don't go near the Ghost House or you will hear:

The clank of a chain
Clank CLANK KERLANK!
A cry of pain
Argh! ARGH! AARRGG HH!

Intended to be read aloud; capitals indicate volume

Mixture of invented sound effects and onomatopoeia

Don't go near the Ghost House. Don't go near!
Don't go near the Ghost House or you will hear:

The rattle of bones
Rittle rattle rittle rattle
The moaning of moans
Moan MoAN MOAN!
The groaning of groans
Groan GrOAN GROAN!

Don't go near the Ghost House. Don't you dare!
The Ghost House is a ghost house
'Cause the Ghost House isn't there!

Surprise at end!

John Foster

TERM 1

Charlotte's Dog

Daniel the spaniel has ears like rugs,
Teeth like prongs of electric plugs.

His back's a thundery winter sky,
Black clouds, white clouds rumbling by.

His nose is the rubber of an old squashed ball
Bounced in the rain. His tail you'd call

A chopped off rope with a motor inside
That keeps it walloping. Red-rimmed-eyed,

He whimpers like plimsolls on a wooden floor.
When he yawns he closes a crimson door.

When he barks it's a shark of a sound that bites
Through frosty mornings and icy nights.

When he sleeps he wheezes on a dozing lung:
Then he wakes you too with a wash of his tongue!

Kit Wright

A list poem

*Each couplet is
independent in the
rhyming scheme*

*Excellent examples of
simile and metaphor*

*Beautiful use of rhythm
in third couplet. What is
the effect of this?*

*Interesting choice of
vocabulary
[WALLOPING]*

*Many accessible similes
and metaphors*

*Couplet six uses the
noun 'shark' as a
subordinate to the
sound, with what
effect?*

SCHOLASTIC

ALL NEW 100 LITERACY HOURS · YEAR 3

Painting with words

1. Write a list of the most important nouns in column 2.
2. Brainstorm adjectives and write these in column 1.
3. Write one phrase in each line telling what the noun is doing (column 3).
4. Start with line 1 and cut out the weakest adjectives from column 1.
5. Work down the column, leaving only one or two adjectives for every line.
6. Read each line and check that you have the best possible phrase at the end of each line.
7. Write a final line that ends the poem with a statement about the subject.

	Adjectives column 1	Nouns column 2	Verb phrase column 3
Line 1			
Line 2			
Line 3			
Line 4			
Line 5			
Final line			

Black Dot

a black dot
a jelly tot

a scum-nail
a jiggle-tail

a cool kicker
a sitting slicker

a panting puffer
a fly-snuffer

a high hopper
a belly-flopper

a catalogue
    To make me

        frog

Libby Houston

Describes the development of the frog from spawn to adult

Begins with four excellent metaphors [VERSES 3 & 4] An image of sophistication reminiscent of The Wind in the Willows

Personification playing amusingly on words appealing to sense of humour and touch [FLY SNUFFER] Reference to the fact that frogs feed on flies

◖**SCHOLASTIC**

UNIT 5

Fact and fiction

In order for children to develop as discerning readers and constructive writers, they need to understand why writers choose different styles and why they organise content in different ways. They must learn to recognise features that characterise different types of writing. They must also learn to 'unpack' and analyse how texts have been crafted. In this unit, children classify a range of texts into fiction and non-fiction. They then discuss the text features and content that led to their decisions. They progress to look at the purpose and organisation of book features such as contents, glossaries, index, bibliographies. Through an analysis of different non-fiction publications, children generate criteria for what constitutes a good read. Finally, children are taught one way of crafting a book review.

The knowledge children gain about general conventions of fiction and non-fiction texts will support learning in later units about the construction of particular types of writing, such as stories, reports and instructions.

Hour	Shared text-level work	Shared word-/ sentence-level work	Guided and independent work	Plenary
1 Librarians at work	Defining fiction and non-fiction and how we distinguish them.		Categorising books into fiction and non-fiction sets; choosing the most interesting.	Sharing lists of titles and presenting choices.
2 Additional book parts	Identifying additional book sections in fiction and non-fiction.		Creating lists and definitions of additional book sections for younger children.	Sharing, discussing and modifying definitions of additional book parts.
3 What makes a good non-fiction read?	Revising definitions of fact, fiction and opinion.	Considering the variety of ways in which texts may be presented.	Considering merits of various publications; identifying important features/sections of non-fiction publications.	Compiling criteria for a good non-fiction book.
4 A good fiction book	Considering the criteria for a good picture story book.	Assessing the importance of punctuation and that every sentence needs a verb.	Identifying verbs in book reviews.	Checking the verbs that were found; talking about interactive nature of reviews.
5 Recommendations	Discussing purpose of book reviews; examining reviews written by other children; identifying powerful adjectives; establishing a review writing frame.		Writing reviews; practising handwriting skills and spelling.	Swapping reviews for evaluation; making amendments as advised.

Key assessment opportunities
● Can the children distinguish between fiction and non-fiction?
● Can they demonstrate their understanding of effective fiction and non-fiction writing by composing effective book reviews?
● Can they produce a piece of writing that is legible, correctly spelled and correctly punctuated?

Librarians at work

Objectives

NLS
T17: To understand the differences in the style and structure of fiction and non-fiction writing.

What you need
● Selection of fiction and non-fiction texts.

Shared text-level work
● Remind the children that libraries tend to categorise books under two main headings: Fiction and Non-fiction. Revise the meanings of these terms and show a novel, a picture story book, an encyclopaedia and a non-fiction book. Examine each book in turn and ask the children to decide whether the book is fiction or non-fiction. Ask how they reached their conclusions without having read the book. What distinctive features helped them to decide? Some of their ideas may be:

● Book titles.
● Content - by opening any page it is clear that a story is being narrated or facts are being shared.
● Headings - in a story book there is generally one title and chapter headings. Non-fiction usually has main headings and many subheadings.
● Illustrations and diagrams - non-fiction is supported by tables, diagrams, photographs and factual sketches. Fiction may be illustrated by paintings or complex line drawings, generally showing characters or setting.
● Page layout - fiction text must be read in order. Non-fiction can often be read in short bursts of information.
● Dialogue - tends not to be used in non-fiction; is frequent in fiction.

● After discussion, the books chosen as being of particular interest should be displayed for general reading.

Guided and independent work
● Tell the children that they are going to organise books for the library. Imagining they are all librarians, tell them first to elect a chief librarian and group scribe. The chief librarian must choose one publication at a time and after group discussion the scribe will write the title in a list headed Fiction or Non-fiction.
● Stress the fact that this is not a guessing game. There must be good reasons for their decisions and you will want them to explain these in the plenary.
● Allow fifteen minutes for this activity and then ask groups to choose one obvious example each of a good fiction and non-fiction publication to show the rest of the class.
● Finally, after further group discussion, ask the scribes to record one general clue that enabled the group to identify fiction texts and one clue or feature that enabled identification of non-fiction texts.

Differentiation

Less able
● Less able children should play the part of chief librarian.

More able
● Children should act as scribe. Perceptive children will mention features such as an index as indicators of non-fiction.

Plenary
● Ask the groups to share their lists and choice of two books with the rest of the class.
● Allow each group in turn, to present their chosen books and identification guides.

Additional book parts

Objectives

NLS
T17: To notice the difference in style and structure of fiction and non-fiction writing.
W13: To collect new words from reading and work in other subjects and create ways of categorising and logging them.

S&L
27 Group discussion and interaction: To use talk to organise roles and action.
31 Group discussion and interaction: To actively include and respond to all members of the group.

What you need
● Sets of fiction and non-fiction books
● photocopiable page 67.

Shared text-level work
● Point out that there are parts to a book besides the main content.
● Show a variety, sharing the sections of a publication that are usually found at the beginning and end – contents, acknowledgements, dedication, copyright, index, glossary, blurb and possibly bibliography.
● Ask the children to point out these parts as you hold open the pages. Consideration of the way in which these book parts enhance the main content should be left for the group discussion.

Guided and independent work
● Organise the children into the same groups as Hour 1 and allocate a chairperson, scribe and timekeeper for each group (or encourage the groups to do this where appropriate). Confirm their functions:

> ● Chairperson – ensures that people take turns, that one person speaks at a time, keeps people on task and ensures by encouragement that everybody participates
> ● Scribe – sets appropriate headings and notes group responses; writing must be swift and legible
> ● Timekeeper – notes time allotted and reminds the group of number of minutes left; this is important when the group becomes stuck on a point and cannot agree.

● Distribute a set of fiction books to half the groups and non-fiction to the other half and ask the children to identify and list additional sections. The chairpersons should choose one book at a time to ensure that the task is carried out methodically. Tell the timekeepers that there is a time limit of twelve minutes for the task.
● After the twelve minutes divide the board in half with column headings Fiction and Non-fiction and take one contribution from each group in turn. Go around the groups until lists are exhausted.
● Tell the children that next they are going to identify the use and organisation of one or two of the additional sections in order to explain them to a younger class.
● Distribute the photocopiable sheet. Discuss the instructions and questions then advise timekeepers of the fifteen minutes to complete the task.

Differentiation

Less able
● Give groups simple features such as acknowledgements and contents to explain.

More able
● The use of glossaries and indexes are the most complex to define. Allocate these to the most able groups of children working on non-fiction.

Plenary
● As each group reports their conclusions, discuss their definitions and amend these if necessary before writing a list for display.
● Using the list, children should point out book parts that are exclusive to fiction and non-fiction and those that are common to both.
● Further work and dynamic consolidation of these ideas could involve children in choosing a publication and explaining the use of additional book sections to a child in a younger class.
● When publishing their own stories and projects, children should be encouraged to incorporate these additional book parts.

What makes a good non-fiction read?

Objectives

NLS
T16: To understand the distinction between fact and fiction; to use terms fact, fiction and non-fiction appropriately.
S9: To notice and investigate a range of other devices for presenting texts.

What you need
● A range of non-fiction texts of varying quality
● photocopiable page 68.

Shared text-level work
● Revise the definitions of fiction and non-fiction and explain that a fact is something that is known to be true. Read the following statements and ask the children whether they are facts or opinions:

● A school is a place where people learn. (F)
● Schools should close at 12 noon. (O)
● All children must attend school by law. (F)
● Children would learn better if each one had a computer on their desk. (O)
● Girls are cleverer than boys. (O)

● Ensure that the children understand that facts usually fit into the genre of non-fiction.
● Tell children that they will be assisting in the selection of library books. A start will be made by considering non-fiction publications, which are based on factual information.

Shared sentence-level work
● Show an example of a non-fiction text with long, unbroken, tightly packed paragraphs of facts and few illustrations. Out-of-date encyclopaedias may provide good examples. Next, show a better publication and ask the children which book they would prefer to read and why. Variety when presenting text is a feature that makes layout interesting. Other examples can be found on the photocopiable sheet.

Guided and independent work
● Distribute sets of non-fiction texts of varying quality. Ask the groups to consider the merits of each book in turn. As books are examined, they should be placed in rank order from the book liked least at the bottom of the pile to the most favoured book at the top. When piles are complete, ask a scribe to list the book titles in order.
● After this discussion, ask the children to write individual lists of features they like and think are important in non-fiction books. Remind the children about additional book sections and encourage them to include these if they feel they are valuable.
● Each member of the group should read one idea from their lists. Ask the scribe to collate an agreed list of ideas for the group.

Differentiation

Less able
● Ask children to write a list of facts about themselves, the school, the classroom or the class topic.

More able
● Ask children to word-process a collated class list for distribution to people who may be involved in selecting and purchasing books for the library or as gifts.

Plenary
● Ask a group spokesperson to read one idea at a time from their lists, then display the lists. Point out that they have drawn up useful criteria for judging a good non-fiction publication.

A good fiction book

Objectives

NLS
T17: To notice differences in the style and structure of fiction and non-fiction writing.
S3: To understand the function of verbs in sentences.
S5: To use the term verb appropriately
S10: To identify the boundaries between separate sentences in reading and in their own writing.

What you need
● An exceptional story book for young children
● photocopiable pages 69.

Shared text-level work
● Use an 'infant' story book in this lesson to ensure that all of the children can engage in critical thinking about fiction.
● Tell the children that they are going to assist Key Stage 1 teachers in selecting fiction for their classes. Read the story, pointing out vivid illustrations and interesting text features such as enlarged or italicised print. Note on the board features that make this publication attractive.
● Distribute photocopiable page 69 and discuss the criteria, adding to the class list as appropriate.
● Suggest that younger children love to be helped and to take advice from more experienced readers, and tell the children that in the next lesson they will have the opportunity to write a fiction or non-fiction book review, recommending a good read.

Shared sentence-level work
● Ask two able children to read out the book reviews on photocopiable page 69. Ask them how they knew when to pause and when to take a breath. Remind everyone about the importance of taking account of punctuation when reading. Ask what punctuation marks identify boundaries between sentences in the first review. (Two exclamation marks and the full stops.) Discuss the use of exclamation marks in a book review and conclude that it gives emphasis. Ask what other punctuation mark can end a sentence. (A question mark.) Elicit that the beginning of a sentence is clearly shown by a capital letter.
● Tell the children that another key feature of a sentence is a verb, without which a sentence can not make sense. Revise the definition and pick out the verbs in the two reviews. In this oral work, mistakes are as useful as correct answers in generating discussion about different parts of speech!

Guided and independent work
● Organise the children into pairs and distribute photocopiable page 68. Ask a good reader in each group to read the first book review for a scribe to list the verbs. Encourage the groups to discuss and correct responses.
● Then tell the reader to read out the second review and ask individuals to extract verbs from this piece of writing.

Differentiation

Less able
● Children should work directly with you while the class works in pairs.

More able
● Encourage children to identify which book they would rather read and explain why.

Plenary
● Identify the verbs and punctuation used in the texts.
● Point out that the purpose of the questions at the beginning of the review is to make the reader think in an interactive way.
● Tell the children that they are going to write a review in the next lesson. Explain that you will provide books but that if they have any favourites they would like to review then they should bring these along to the next lesson.

Recommendations

Objectives

NLS
T17: To notice the difference in style and structure of fiction and non-fiction writing.
T22: To write simple non-chronological reports, using notes made to organise and present ideas. Write for a known audience.
W3: To read and spell correctly the high-frequency words from KS1.
W20: To practise the correct formation of basic joins from Year 2

What you need
● Variety of good-quality non-fiction and fiction books
● photocopiable pages 68 and 69
● high-frequency word lists.

Shared text-level work

● Discuss the purpose of writing book reviews. There are huge numbers of publications to choose from and people often seek recommendations from others to help in choosing a book. Written recommendations may be shared with a wide audience and can be found in the bookshop, in magazines and newspapers and on websites.

● Tell the children that they are going to review a book that they value very highly and would recommend to readers like themselves.

● Re-read the second non-fiction review on photocopiable page 68 and point out that the reviewers have compared the publication against the criteria. They probably read the book and then ticked the list. Then they would have noted points from the list in sentences. These points have then been organised in a logical order to create a paragraph.

● Examine the strong adjectives used to persuade the reader that this book is a good read: *amazing, excellent, boredom-busting, exciting, brightly coloured.*

● Tell the children that they will be following this process for reviewing a book of their choice. Write the following instructions on the board:

> ● Read the book.
> ● Scrutinise illustrations/diagrams.
> ● Tick criteria that apply to the publication.
> ● Write a phrase or sentence about the main criteria.
> ● Use sentences to craft a paragraph telling the good points about the book.
> ● Include strong adjectives that will convince the reader that he or she will like this book.

Guided and independent work

● Tell the children to choose a book to review (either fiction or non-fiction). Allow thirty minutes for reading and rough drafting.

● Remind the children of horizontal and diagonal joins between letters in their handwriting, with and without ascenders. Spend a few minutes revising these and allow time for practice.

● Also remind children of the importance of correct spellings to go with this beautiful handwriting, to ensure that the intended audience can read the reviews.

● Display high-frequency word lists and ask the children to check that all of these words are correctly spelled in their reviews.

Differentiation

Less able
● Ask children to make a poster advertising their chosen book rather than writing the review.

More able
● Children could publish their reviews on a site like Amazon.

Plenary

● Ask the children to swap self-corrected reviews with a partner who should correct any other obvious errors in spelling and punctuation. The partners should also tell each other if the reviews interested them and would make them want to read the book. Encourage them to advise on any improvements needed.

● Reviews should be amended accordingly and then copied using good-quality writing materials. These should be folded into envelopes and fixed in the books for prospective readers to read when choosing books.

Additional book parts

1. Name/title of additional book section:

_____

2. In what part of the book is this section found?

_____

3. Why do you think this section is included in the book?

_____

4. How is this section organised?

_____

◼ Tick if it is a:

- list ☐
- couple of sentences ☐
- paragraph ☐
- few paragraphs. ☐

◼ Use the notes above to explain the purpose and organisation of the book part. Be as clear as possible so that a younger child will understand.

Definition

A [name of book part] _____

can be found at [Explain in what part of the book it will be found]

_____

_____

The reader uses this section to

_____

_____

This additional part of the book is written in

_____

Non-fiction we like

Criteria for what makes a good non-fiction book
List generated by the children of Fintry Primary School

About an interesting subject

The sort of information that makes a subject interesting

Bits of information that are not too long

'Did you know?' sections

Quiz corners

Catchy title

Attractive cover

Index page

Glossary

Bright illustrations

Easy-to-understand facts

Funny facts

Facts presented in different ways

Fun things to do or read

Well set-out pages

Flaps and parts that move

Not long and boring – punchy

Easy to understand

True/realistic

Eye-catching

Diagrams and colour keys

A good price

Reviews

Until I Met Dudley by Roger McGough and Chris Riddell
Until I Met Dudley gives young children a good grasp on how household appliances are worked, used and built. At the same time Chris Riddell's amazing artwork makes learning fun and creative, especially in the pages where he draws the girls' imaginative mechanical machine. In the book Roger McGough, or Dudley, teaches you how the machines in your house work and how the insides look. The book wasn't only one of the favourite publications in our class, it was also runner up for the English Association four-eleven award for the best children's picture book of the year. We rate this an excellent book!

Review by Ryan Sims, Adam Mundell and Tom Stearns, Fintry Primary School

200 Boredom Busters by Paul Scott
Missing your school pals? Too wet to play? Suffering from boredom during the long summer holiday?

Well not any more with this boredom-busting book! Packed full of the most exciting things to do, from page 1 to 91 this book explodes with things to do on rainy days. Paul Scott has done a great job of compiling a book filled with fun things to do, like making a Mexican hat or fingering the culprit. The problem with this book is how to choose when every page you turn is more fascinating than the last. Brightly coloured illustrations and photographs make instructions clear.

So say goodbye to boredom and say a great hello to 2000 Boredom Busters! I give this book a big thumbs up!

Review by Emma Howarth

▬ SCHOLASTIC

Fiction young children like

List generated by the junior children of Fintry Primary School

Good story

Story that is funny

Story that is frightening

Adventure stories

Story with things that are repeated

Animal characters

Fairytale characters

Cartoon characters

Real people, but must be interesting

Happy ending

Not too many words

Places that are exciting

Places in the imagination

Big writing

Different sizes of writing

Colourful pictures

Black and white pictures with a lot of detail

Interesting chapter headings

An interesting title and a bright cover

Cheap price

Parts that jump out and lift up

Six Dinner Sid
by Inga Moore
All young children will love Sid, the main character in this book because he is such a chancer! He pretends that he lives in six different houses! A cat could get away with this trick because they always do what they want to. Find out how Sid gets caught out by reading this funny story. There are a lot of lovely pictures in this book that young children can look at by themselves once they know the story. The book has a happy ending. This book has won many awards.

Review by Shona Jenkins and Francesca Irvine, Fintry Primary School

---

Omnibombulator

by Dick King-Smith
This is the story of a very small beetle with a very big name. Young children will like this book because it is about a creature that nobody cares about and is ignored because it is so small. Sometimes young children feel like that. Omnibombulator has a lot of adventures and many escapes and in the end meets another character that likes him. There are interesting chapter headings in this book that make you want to read the next one. The pictures are just black and white but they are funny and interesting. There is a happy ending.

Review by Jamie Smith and William Aitken, Fintry Primary School

---

UNIT 6

Reports

When learning how to read, interpret and then write reports, children must first revise what they know about non-fiction texts. They will also discover that depending upon purpose and audience, non-fiction texts differ in the way in which information is presented. Children learn how to structure a report using economical, factual prose. They also learn how to lay out the text on the page. One of the most difficult parts of this process is in taking information from one or two texts and presenting it in a new way. This unit gives children the opportunity of publishing their own reference book on the topic of birds (making links to science and PSHE). Each child will require a thin jotter or booklet. The first pages should be left blank for a contents list. Thereafter there will be four reports, followed by an index and glossary. There is scope for enriching the publication with other genre writing such as bird poetry, accounts of bird watching, and instructions for making a bird table. The reference book outcome is highly motivating; however it is possible to carry out the lessons, omitting the publishing ideas.

The unit, particularly Hour 4, covers objectives in *Grammar for Writing* Unit 9.

Hour	Shared text-level work	Shared word-/ sentence-level work	Guided and independent work	Plenary
1 What is a report?	Establishing what to research for topic on birds; discussing presentation styles.	Inferring the meaning of unknown words from context.	Choosing six main points of information for younger audience.	Discussing and justifying selections.
2 Interesting pages	Exploring ways of classifying information.	Investigating different ways of presenting text; use of commas in lists.	Transferring information from a table to sentences as the first page in topic book/report; evaluating spreads in non-fiction books.	Sharing criteria for good information texts/reports.
3 Creating a double-page spread		Splitting words into syllables for spelling; revising topic vocabulary; using dictionaries.	Designing double-page spreads.	Assessing each other's work against agreed criteria.
4 Bird watchers' reports	Reading and studying birdwatchers' reports.	Exploring the *re* prefix.	Compiling topic reports; practising handwriting.	Sharing reports; examining different presentation methods.
5 Publication	Discussing uses and layouts of glossary, index and contents pages.	Organising a glossary.	Completing pages for individual report books; adding covers.	Reviewing the topic; publishing/displaying the topic books.

Key assessment opportunities
● Do the children use commas correctly when writing lists?
● Can they spell specialist terminology correctly?
● Can they write a coherent report?
● Do they understand the purpose and conventions for organising an index, glossary and contents?

What is a report?

Objectives

NLS
T21: To read information passages and identify main points... noting key words or phrases, listing key points.
W14: To infer the meaning of unknown words from context.

What you need
● Photocopiable page 70.

Shared text-level work
● Tell the children that they are going to write and illustrate a book for Key Stage 1 children on the topic of birds. They will be involved in finding information and writing and illustrating reports. Explain that their publications will have glossaries, indexes and contents enabling young readers to find subjects of particular interest.
● Like professional authors, children will research their subject first. Discuss that before beginning research it is useful to establish what we already know and note the questions to which we want answers.
● Divide a flip chart sheet in half with the headings: Things we already know about birds and Questions about birds. Establish and note facts already known. Then record questions the children would like answered, such as *Do birds sleep lying down? Can all birds fly? Why do birds sing?*
● Remind the children that the information they will present in their bird books will be written in the form of reports. Explain that the information on the photocopiable sheet has been written for Year 3 children and will have to be simplified for younger children.
● Read through the report. Then, as you re-read, discuss any suggestions the children can offer on features of style and presentation that characterise a report. For example:

> ● The report is full of facts.
> ● It is written in the present tense.
> ● The language is straightforward.
> ● Unlike instruction writing or a story, the chronological order of the information is not important.

Shared word-level work
● Ask the children if they can guess the meaning of the words *habitat, scavenger, prey* and *migrate.* Ask how they worked out the meanings. Remind them that when researching they will sometimes come across words they do not understand and one of the ways to have an idea of the meaning is to read around the word and consider what it could mean in its context.

Guided and independent work
● Ask the children to select (by highlighting or underlining) six main points of information from the report that they think will interest younger children. Explain that choosing only six points will be difficult, but that Key Stage 1 children are only able to cope with small amounts of information at one time.

Differentiation

Less able
● Children should not be restricted on the number of main points chosen.

More able
● Children should compare their chosen pieces of information with their partners'.

Plenary
● Ask the children to read and justify one of their chosen pieces of information. There are no wrong answers, but there may be interesting debate about the relative importance of information selected.
● Add the photocopied sheets to the display with the flip chart sheets. Let children compare the different information selected.

Interesting pages

Objectives

NLS
T19: To compare the way information is presented.
S9: To notice and investigate a range of other devices for presenting texts.
S13: To use commas to separate items in a list

What you need
● Variety of non-fiction books (not about birds)
● the children's bird books.

Shared text-level work
● Tell the children that they are going to create the first page of their bird book. Copy the following table on the board or OHT. (Encourage the children to contribute if possible.)

Bird and their habitats

Gardens	Open country	Woodland	Open water
Blackbird	Lark	Woodpecker	Grebe
Thrush	Pipit	Fly catcher	Diving duck
Wren	Partridge	Woodcock	Swan
Chaffinch	Curlew	Tawny owl	Gannet

● Explain that there are many ways of organising living creatures into groups. These groups are called classes and the act of organising is called classifying. One way of classifying birds is according to habitat. Point out that the table above features only some of the most common habitats and birds.

Shared sentence-level work
● Tell the children that a table is only one way of representing information about bird habitats. In their bird books, tell the children to put the information in the table into sentences. Model the process on the board by writing a sentence about garden birds: The *blackbird, thrush, wren* and *chaffinch* may be found in gardens.
● Ask a volunteer to give a sentence orally about open country birds. Write this on the board, leaving out the commas. Ask what is missing and explain the use of commas when writing a list in a sentence.
● Emphasise the inclusion of the word *and* before the final item in the list. Ask the children what the last two sentences in this section will be.

Guided and independent work
● Under the heading 'Bird habitats', ask the children to write four sentences to begin their bird book. Remind them to leave a page for the contents that will be completed later. Stress the importance of correct spelling and handwriting in a book to be read by younger children.
● Allow fifteen minutes for this task. Distribute non-fiction texts to groups of four children. These should not be bird books so the children realise that their learning is transferable.
● Ask the children to choose a good double-page spread. Tell them to use this spread to analyse how reports can be presented to make non-fiction clear and interesting. Ask them to discuss the question *How has the writer/illustrator/publisher created an interesting page?* Individually, children should write five statements in answer to the question.

Plenary
● Share the criteria for a good non-fiction double-page spread and draw up a list to add to the display. Check this against photocopiable page 68 in Unit 5.

Differentiation

Less able
● Ask children to write two answer statements.

More able
● Ask children to write seven answer statements.

Creating a double-page spread

Objectives

NLS
T19: To compare the way information is presented.
S9: To notice and investigate a range of devices for presenting texts.
W4: To discriminate syllables in reading and spelling.
W15: To have a secure understanding of the purpose and organisation of the dictionary.

What you need
- Highlighted photocopiable page 76
- dictionaries
- leaflets, books, posters and photographs of birds
- the children's bird books
- art materials
- large Post-it Notes.

Shared word-level work
- Write the following words on a large sheet of paper: bird, feather, tail, fly, eat, song, habitat, scavenger, prey, migrate.
- Tell the children that these will be used a great deal in project writing and their spellings must be learned by heart. Split long words into syllables and show the children how this can inform correct spelling when the word is re-assembled: hab-it-at, scav-en-ger.
- Ask the children to copy the list for learning at home by Look-Say-Cover-Write-Check.
- Now ask the children if they remember the meanings of the words *habitat, scavenger, prey* and *migrate* from the first lesson. Check their answers in a dictionary, taking prompts from the children on how the dictionary is organised and how to find words.
- Recap that dictionaries can be used for checking spelling and for finding out the meanings of words. Add definitions to the words on the large sheet of paper.
- Distribute six dictionaries and ask six children to go away and look up the meaning of the remaining six words in the spelling list and record the definitions. While this is being done, discuss the meaning of the words with the rest of the class. Compare these definitions with the dictionary definitions. Add agreed definitions to the sheet.

Guided and independent work
- Organise working groups and ask the children to design a double-page spread in their bird books.
- Explain that they should use the main points about birds they selected in Hour 1. Tell them to write each point as a short report and to illustrate the report. Refer to the list of criteria for a good double-page spread drawn up in Hour 2 and discuss each point, encouraging children to consider how they will meet the criteria in their own publication. At this stage, make available information to help with illustrations and distribute highlighted photocopiable page 76. Although the children are designing and writing their own pages, they should support one another in groups.

Differentiation

Less able
- Tell children to draw a picture of a bird in the middle of the page and to write their facts in boxes around it.

More able
- Children should use all of the statements they identified in Hour 1.

Plenary
- With permission, choose one of the children's double-page spreads and demonstrate how to assess this against the criteria.
- Ask the children to place their open books in a large circle around the classroom. Give every child a Post-it Note and then ask them to move in a circle looking at every book in turn. Stop the assessment carousel (at any point) and ask every child to write on the Post-it a positive comment on the book in front of them. Tell them to sign their comment and attach the note to the book for the author to see.

Bird watchers' reports

Objectives

NLS
T18: To locate information using subheadings.
T21: To make a simple record of information from texts read.
T22: To write simple non-chronological reports from texts read.
W10 To recognise and spell common prefixes and how these influence word meanings.

What you need
● Photocopiable pages 77 and 78
● writing frames based on photocopiable page 77
● the children's bird books.

Shared text-level work
● Show the children photocopiable page 77. The text shows the way in which reports on birds are generally organised in books for bird watchers. The purpose of these books is to enable readers to find information quickly, either to identify birds or find out more details about them. The text on page 78 gives information in a different format. Tell the children that they are going to transfer that information to the report format found in bird watcher's guidebooks.
● Ask the children to read out the subheadings on photocopiable page 77 for you to write on the board.
● Read 'The robin' with the children and then scan the text for the headings on the board, adding information in similar format to page 76. Suggest that as each piece of information is located, it should be crossed through so that the researcher does not have to re-read information that has already been 'used'. Children will notice after this that there is information remaining on the sheet that will not be transferred to the shorthand report form. This is because impersonal, non-chronological reports should not feature stories, recounts of personal experiences or the opinions of the writer. Clear the board before continuing.

Shared word-level work
● Tell the children that they are going to rewrite the information in the diaries as reports. Take the opportunity to explore the *re* prefix. Write the words *rewritten* and *rewrite* on the board and tell the children that the *re* prefix means *again,* so there is the opportunity to start again and improve the first draft of a text in sentence construction as well as spelling and presentation.
● Ask for other examples of the use of *re*, for example, *re-run the race, return to the house, reorganise the furniture, revise the work, replay the match.*

Guided and independent work
● Distribute the writing frames and ask the children to compile reports on the robin and golden eagle before rewriting them in their bird books.
● Stress the importance of ensuring that handwritten letters are of a consistent size and that spaces between letters and words are also consistent to ensure handwriting is neat and legible.

Differentiation

Less able
● Children should complete the report on the robin, which has been modelled.

More able
● Children should choose and research another bird on the internet or in the library to produce a report on a third bird.

Plenary
● Ask the children to number the pages of their bird books beginning with the first report as page 1. Tell the children that they may choose where on the page to place the numbers but this must remain consistent throughout the book.
● In numbering pages and looking through the books, point out the different ways in which material about birds has been presented and remind the children that all of these are effective ways of writing and presenting reports.

Publication

Objectives

NLS
T18: To locate information using contents, index, headings, page numbers.
W13: To collect new words from reading and work in other subjects.

What you need
● The children's bird books
● art materials
● non-fiction books with contents, glossaries and indexes.

Shared text- and word-level work
● Tell the children that in order to complete their bird books, they will organise glossaries to help their readers understand specialist vocabulary, indexes to help them find particular information and contents to find broader topics.
● Ask the children to suggest where in the book to place these sections. (The index will fit on the last two pages and the glossary on the page before that; the contents at the front.)
● Show an index and note that it is organised in an alphabetical list. Establish that the numbers next to the words tell us on what page(s) the information can be found. List the birds that appear in the children's books. With the children's help, reorganise them into an alphabetical list.
● Ask the children to copy the index onto the last two pages of their books and to add the relevant page numbers.
● Now organise the glossary. This too will be organised alphabetically, on the page before the index. (The glossary should consist of the topic spelling list with the definitions listed in Hour 3.)
● Next, compile the contents page. Show the children contents pages from a few books to remind them of its function and how the text is presented. Go through one of the children's books, demonstrating how page headings should be copied into the contents list at the front of the book. Page numbers will then need to be added next to the headings.
● Finally, discuss the task of designing a cover. Examine some non-fiction covers and elicit the information that must be included along with an illustration.

Guided and independent work
● Ask the children to complete their additional pages individually but encourage them to discuss their work with their peers.
● When several children have finished, group them together to work on their covers. Remind them to write the book title and author's name, remembering to include capital letters where appropriate.
● Finally, in pairs, children should check their partner's contents and index pages to ensure that they are correct. The covers could be produced using ICT.

Plenary
● Review the topic and discuss other subjects about which the children may like to publish books.
● In addition to displaying the books, finish the unit with some of the following activities:

● Taking the books home to be reviewed by parents and read to younger siblings.
● Reading their book to a younger class.
● Reviewing a peer publication.
● Organising a book launch with parents/friends/other visitors.

Differentiation

Less able
● Children should not be required to produce an index or glossary.

More able
● Ask children to write peer book reviews to be inserted in an envelope attached to the publication.

Birds

Birds are warm-blooded animals that lay eggs. Their bodies are covered with feathers and instead of arms, they have wings. In most types of bird, wings are used for flying. Some birds, however, because of the place they live or because they have become too heavy, have lost the ability to fly. The habitat of the ostrich, which is vast open plains, has encouraged this bird to develop powerful legs for running, while its wings have become very small and ineffective.

Some birds eat seeds and nuts, some eat insects and some even hunt other birds! Some birds like to eat things left behind by others, such as food left behind after picnics or even the putrid leftovers from the meals of hunting birds. Vultures eat dead bodies! These scavengers must have very strong stomachs!

Some birds, like the blackbird, stay in Britain all year round. Others, like the swallow and the osprey, migrate and spend our cold winter months in warmer countries in the south.

Birdwatcher's guide

Tawny owl

Appearance   The tawny owl and the barn owl are the most well-known owls in Britain. The plumage is rich brown, marked with light and dark bars and streaks. The female is larger than the male.

Habitat   Woodland and trees

Nest   Built from decayed wood, pellets and feathers. Built in a hole in a tree or building ruins, or in the old nest of a crow or pigeon or other large bird.

Eggs   3 or 4, white

Food   Rats, mice, small birds, young game, rabbits and insects

Sounds   "Tu-whit", "whit" and the long, wavering, eerie call, "Ho-hoo-hooooo".

Length   38cm

TERM 1

Birdwatchers' diaries

The robin

I have a bird table in my garden and the bird that visits me every day all year round is the robin. It is not the least bit afraid of me and comes very close when I am gardening. The robin is small, about 14cm long. It has light-brown plumage with a bright red breast. A story in some countries tells that the robin got its red breast when a spot of blood dripped onto it when trying to remove the nail from Jesus' hand during the crucifixion. The robin hunts for insects of all kinds around the roots of bushes and small trees. It builds its nest of grass, wool, moss and animal hair in a hole in a tree or a wall or sometimes in barns or churches. Last year I went to fill a hole in my garden wall and found the robin's nest. I looked very carefully into the nest and saw six white eggs speckled all over with light red. I had to leave the hole in the wall! Besides living in gardens, robins live in parks, hedgerows and woods. I love to hear the robin singing in my garden. It has a thin warbling song which sounds like "tic-tic" and sometimes "tsit" and a high-pitched "tswee".

Golden eagle

When I was in the Highlands of Scotland last year I was amazed to see a golden eagle circling in the sky. It was looking for something to eat. Eagles eat rabbits, hares, grouse, rats and even small lambs. I sat and watched the eagle circling and looking for prey for about an hour. The eagle's long, broad wings enable it to stay in the air for hours while it hunts. I knew that somewhere in those high mountain crags, the eagle would have its nest. They build large nests from sticks, heather and grass. The eagle's call sent a shiver down my spine. It sounds like a shrill yelp or bark. I couldn't believe how huge the eagle was. From its head to the tip of its tail it must have measured three feet (82cm). The eagle was mostly dark brown and I could see that only its head and neck were golden. Golden eagles usually lay two eggs which are white with blotches of red and brown. The eagle was so beautiful. I wished I could have painted a picture of him.

◼ S C H O L A S T I C

UNIT 1

Narrative: themes

This unit covers traditional stories. Lessons focus on typical themes and features of parables, fairy tales, fables, myths and legends, often making links to PSHE and citizenship. Story structure and language are considered, as well as characterisation. There are concerns that in the space of an hour it is impossible for young children to complete extended pieces of writing. In the second half of this unit, there are five connected lessons which give the opportunity for children to plan and write an extended story for publication. Before embarking on this unit, children should be told that they are going to be studying well-loved stories that have been told to people across the world for hundreds of years. Show the children some good-quality publications and tell them that not only are these great stories but the illustrations, beautiful print, decorated borders and even the paper make them a joy to read.

To publish the children's legends you could use:
- Plain or lined A4 with A4 card cover. Children write on one side of the paper.
- Pieces are stapled along the top when whole book is complete.
- As above but stapled along one side. Plenty of space must be left for stapling.
- As above but held together with a spine or sewn with thick thread
- A zig-zag book made with cartridge paper. Be sure to leave front page for cover and dedication. Long pieces of writing may continue along the back of the zig-zag.

Hour	Shared text-level work	Shared word-/ sentence-level work	Guided and independent work	Plenary
1 Fables	Telling the stories of 'The Boy Who Cried Wolf' and 'Matilda'.	Examining use of punctuation in the poem; splitting words into syllables.	Reciting the poem; defining fable.	Discussing definitions; talking about other fables.
2 Parables	Telling the parable of 'The Good Samaritan'.		Develop and dramatise a modern version of the parable; defining parable.	Discussing dramas; comparing definitions.
3 Myths and legends	Reading a myth and a legend.		Dividing a story into sections/ paragraphs; illustrating the story sections to create storyboards.	Displaying storyboards to tell story; defining myth and legend.
4 Goodies or baddies?	Analysing famous story characters.		Brainstorming bad and good characters; describing them in a paragraph.	Categorising characters; sharing descriptions to identify characteristics.
5 Police letters	Using the form of a letter to build character descriptions.		Writing a letter to describe a fairy tale character.	Reading the letters and identifying the characters.

UNIT 1

Hour	Shared text-level work	Shared word-/ sentence-level work	Guided reading/ writing	Independent work	Plenary
6 The Code of Chivalry	Telling the story of 'The Sword in the Stone'; discussing knights and the Code of Chivalry.	Exploring opposites to help with understanding; exploring prefixes.	Drawing up own list of knightly virtues.	Discussing main virtues; thinking about knightly adventures.	Matching word cards to words on the board. Identifying sounds with various spellings.
7 Knights of the new millennium	Brainstorming ideas for 21st-century knights' adventures.		Drafting character-description introductions to own stories.	Reading story introductions.	Sharing couplets. Focusing on long-vowel digraphs and rhymes.
8 A story worth telling	Talking about publishing their stories, including dedication and prologue.	Correcting descriptions from Hour 7.	Adding corrected words to spelling books; rewriting the prologue; telling stories orally.	Choosing people for dedications.	Reading and discussing new verses, focusing on rhyme.
9 Authors at work	Establishing children's story 'book' structure and tasks.	Practising diagonal joins in handwriting.	Writing their stories; checking progress to correct where necessary.	Reading stories.	Discussing different uses of capital letters.
10 The new millennium knights	Shared design of a front cover and writing dedication.	Checking how to write with consistent size; revising use of capital letters for names and titles.	Completing their new-legend stories.	Discussing story themes; arranging a book launch.	Sharing poems, focusing on spelling and discussing how punctuation affects reading.

Key assessment opportunities
● Can the children tell the difference between a myth, a legend, a fable and a parable?
● Do they know the conventions for laying out a letter?
● Can they write a coherent paragraph of character description?
● Can they imagine and tell a coherent story with an identifiable theme?
● Do they self-correct most mistakes?

Fables

Objectives

NLS

T2: To identify typical story themes.
T4: To prepare poems for performance.
S6: To note where commas occur in reading and to discus their functions in helping the reader.
W4: To discriminate syllables in reading and spelling.

S&L

29 Speaking: To prepare poems for performance.

What you need
● Photocopiable page 91
● definition of fable for display.

Shared text-level work
● Tell the story of 'The Boy Who Cried Wolf' and ask why this gory tale is told to children. (To emphasise the importance of telling the truth.)

> Once there was a boy who tended the sheep for his parents. He thought it was a good joke every now and then to shout, 'Wolf! Wolf!' to make everyone panic and run up the mountain. The parents became angry with him until eventually when they heard him shouting, they would just wander to the door to check. They guessed he would be joking.
>
> One day, the boy's parents heard him calling frantically, "Wolf! Wolf!" They knew he would be joking, so they didn't even interrupt their meal to have a look.
>
> That evening, the boy didn't come home, and when his parents went to look for him, they found only bones...

● Read 'Matilda' and ask the children to consider the message of the poem. Add the missing final lines:
Matilda
Who told Lies and was Burned to Death.
● Re-read the first eight lines to demonstrate how the punctuation helps to keep the rhythm and communicate meaning.

Shared sentence- and word-level work
● Ask the children what the comma is used for. (To indicate a short pause.) Point out the semicolon and explain that this separates parts of a sentence and indicates a pause that is longer than a comma but shorter than a full stop.
● Clap the beats in the first line of the poem and explain that the beats of a word are called syllables. Splitting long words into their syllables can be helpful when reading and spelling. For example, the word *attempted*, when split into three syllables reminds us that there are two *t*s at the beginning of the word, *at-tempt-ed*.
● Ask why the poet has written capital letters at the beginning of words in the middle of lines. (These words are emphasised.)
● Explain that the two stories are fables. Discuss similarities in the characters and their actions, and ask groups to write a definition of this type of story.

Differentiation

Less able
● Allocate three lines and rehearse these lines with the children.

More able
● Challenge children to find more examples in the library or on the internet, for sharing at story time.

Guided and independent work
● Divide the class into groups of five or six and give one part of the poem to each group. Tell the children they have five minutes to practise, and afterwards recite the poem with emphasis and expression!

Plenary
● Ask each group to read out their definition of a fable. Show them yours and display all of the definitions together.
● Discuss other examples of fables, including familiar ones from Aesop.

UNIT 1 HOUR 2 ◾ Narrative: themes

Parables

Objectives

NLS
T2: To identify typical story themes.
T9: To write a story plan for own fable or traditional tale, using story theme from reading but substituting different characters or changing the setting.
W20: To write their own definitions of words.

S&L
29 Speaking: To choose and prepare stories for performance.
32 Drama: To identify and discuss qualities of others' performances.

What you need
● Definition of parable for display
● examples of parables.

Shared text-level work
● Tell the children that they are going to study parables. Explain that the story of 'The Good Samaritan' is a parable that Jesus told, and read the following version.

> A man was attacked by thieves, beaten up, robbed and left to bleed at the side of the road. Numerous people looked at the dying man and walked on, too busy and too important to waste their time with a person who was in such a mess! A man from Samaria came along. People from his country were called Samaritans. He was in a hurry but he stopped anyway and carried the man to a hospital. The people at the hospital wouldn't let him in because he hadn't any money to pay for treatment. The Samaritan gave the hospital sufficient money to take care of the man and went about his business.

Guided and independent work
● Organise the children into groups of six and tell them that they are going to dramatise a modern-day 'The Good Samaritan' parable.
● Write the following questions for the children to consider:

> ● Where is the setting?
> ● Who is the person who is attacked?
> ● Who are the people who attack him/her? Why?
> ● Why don't other people help?
> ● Where does the Samaritan come from?
> ● Why does s/he decide to help?

● The children will also have to decide upon which parts to play:

> ● two thieves – they can also play the hospital staff
> ● two people who walk by
> ● Good Samaritan
> ● person who is attacked.

● Allow ten minutes for questions to be discussed and characters and roles decided. Advise the children that their plays should last for no longer than three minutes.
● Allow five to ten minutes for rehearsal. Remind the children that modern titles will be used and announced before the plays begin.
● Watch the group performances and encourage positive comments from the audience.
● Now ask the drama groups to write a definition of this type of story: *A parable is a story that...*

Differentiation

Less able
● Children should rehearse their lines for you before the performance.

More able
● Ask children to write out the playscript.

Plenary
● Talk about the performances. How well were they updated?
● Compare the children's definitions with the one you have written, and add them to the display.
● Elicit the moral from the parable. (Always help people in need.)
● Read and talk about a few more short examples of parables.

Myths and legends

Objectives

NLS
T7: To describe and sequence key incidents in a variety of ways, eg by making simple storyboards.
W17: To continue the collection of new words from reading.

What you need

● Photocopiable pages 92 and 93
● cartridge paper and art materials.

Shared text-level work

● Tell the children that you are going to tell them two stories. One of the stories is a myth and the other is a legend, and they will have to decide which is which.
● Read the stories on photocopiable pages 92 and 93. Briefly talk about reactions, the settings and characters, but avoid genre discussion at this stage.
● Tell children that they will be retelling one of the stories and adding an illustration.

Guided and independent work

● Organise groups of five, with a chairperson, scribe and timekeeper appointed in each group. Tell the children which story they will be responsible for and distribute photocopiable pages as appropriate.
● Ask the children to split the story into five story sections. Tell them to read the full story first, then mark the separate sections by underlining or highlighting each one in a different colour.
● Compare the results for each story, asking groups responsible for the other story to comment on the decisions made. This will no doubt provoke lively discussion.
● Tell the children that there are no absolutely correct answers but they need to justify their choices. If sections are very wrong then you should intervene with an explanation that a new paragraph/section should be started when there is a change of subject or tone in the story or when time moves on.
● Using a new copy of their story, ask groups to cut up the sections and divide these around the group.
● Distribute A4 cartridge paper and art materials and ask the children to illustrate their part of the story.

Plenary

● Explain to the children that they have created storyboards. When they are displayed together they tell the whole story.
● Remind the children that one of these stories is a myth and the other a legend. Ask how the stories are similar and how they are different.
● Explain that both myths and legends can be stories of heroic victories over fearsome creatures. However, a myth is about an invented character in a fiction that addresses grand themes of the world, and a legend is about a more down-to-earth character who actually existed. A legend is a story that has some truth in it but that has been exaggerated over the centuries.
● Establish that the story of 'George and the Dragon' is the legend (St George, in some form, is a figure from history), whereas Beowulf and Grendel are mythical characters.
● Drawing on the children's knowledge, discuss other famous figures from myth and legend to reinforce this distinction, such as Odysseus, Robin Hood, King Arthur, King Alfred, King Canute and William Wallace.

Differentiation

Less able
● Point out to the children that the story can be divided according to the line breaks.

More able
● Children should research further examples of myths and legends, and share these with the class.

▢ **83**

UNIT 1 HOUR 4 Narrative: themes

Goodies or baddies?

Objectives

NLS
T3 To identify and discuss main and recurring characters, evaluate their behaviour and justify views.
W6: To use independent spelling strategies.
W19: To use dictionaries to learn or check the spellings of words.

What you need
● Dictionaries.

Shared text-level work
● Tell the children that they are going to analyse some of the characters we meet in traditional stories, starting with:

> ● St George from 'George and the Dragon'
> ● Beauty from 'Beauty and the Beast'
> ● the Witch from 'Hansel and Gretel'.

● Taking each character in turn, go through questions like these:

> ● What does the character look like?
> ● What does s/he wear?
> ● Is this character young, middle-aged or old?
> ● Is this character poor or rich?
> ● Is s/he magic?
> ● Is s/he Royal?
> ● What things does s/he do or say that tell you s/he is good or evil?
> ● What happens to the character at the end of the story?
> ● Would you like to meet this character? Why?

● Ask the children to answer orally in sentences and explain that if these answers were written together they would form a paragraph of character description.

Guided and independent work
● Organise the children into groups with a chairperson, scribe and timekeeper and ask the children to brainstorm good and bad characters they know from traditional stories.
● After ten minutes, tell the children to choose their favourite 'good' character and character of whom they are most scared.
● After sharing these choices, tell each child which to write about, to ensure there is a balance of good and evil characters to display.
● Ask the children to write their character descriptions.
● Tell the children that as this work is for display they should try to spell words correctly as they write, using independent strategies or checking in the dictionary.

Plenary
● Ask volunteers from each group to read their character descriptions and include them in a display under the headings Goodies or Baddies.
● Discuss that most characters in traditional stories are very clearly either bad or good, as this 'conflict' is one of the key themes of this type of story. One of the characters difficult to categorise is the woodcutter in *Snow White*. At first, he was clearly a baddie but later he found it impossible to kill Snow White, even though his evil boss told him to. He then became a good character. Remind the children that in the stories they read, there are a few characters who struggle with being good or bad. Look at the characters in each section of the display and discuss the characteristics they have in common.

Differentiation

Less able
● Children should answer only the first five questions.

More able
● Children should choose another character in the story and write down what s/he thinks about their chosen person.

Police letters

Objectives

NLS
T3: To identify and discuss main and recurring characters, evaluate their behaviour and justify views.
T8: To write portraits of characters using story text to describe behaviour and characteristics and presenting portraits in a variety of ways.

Shared text-level work

● Tell the children a 'tall tale' that recently you were stuck in a lift with a young girl who told you that she was running away from a wicked aunt who had attempted to have her killed!
● Say to the class that you feel obliged to report this and have written the following letter:

Dear Constable

On Monday, I was stuck in a lift for three hours with a girl who told me that her aunt tried to have her killed last year! She said that her aunt is jealous of her. She is living with seven people who work as woodchoppers. She cleans and cooks for them and in return they give her a room and all her food. She said that these people are very kind to her. She is frightened in case her aunt finds her. I am worried about this girl. She wouldn't tell me her name but she has long, dark hair, large brown eyes and very pale skin. She was wearing a pretty but old-fashioned dress. She lives in the Deep Dark Wood. Would you please investigate this matter?

Yours sincerely

Ms/Mr X

● Ask the children what they would write in a letter to the police if they had been stuck in the lift with an evil character, such as Rumpelstiltskin.
● Work together to build up a letter similar to the one above.

Guided and independent work

● Revise the rules for laying out a letter and then ask the children to make their own choice of character they encounter in the lift. Specify that it must be a character from a fairy tale. (This narrows the choice and gives other children a chance to guess who the character is.)
● Brainstorm some popular fairy tales and characters to refresh the children's memories.
● Stress that the children must keep their characters secret from the rest of the class.
● Tell the children to write their letters describing the character and to fold up a flap at the bottom of the page. On the outside of the flap it should say, *Who was stuck in the lift?* Under the flap, they should write the name of the character.

Differentiation

Less able
● Using ideas on the board about Rumpelstiltskin, give children a writing frame to write an appropriate letter.

More able
● Ask children to write a letter of thanks from the police, having investigated the case.

Plenary

● Ask a few children to read out their letters and allow the rest of the class to guess who the character is.
● Display final drafts of the letters for reading and guessing.

The Code of Chivalry

Objectives

NLS
T2: To identify typical story themes.
W17: To continue the collection of new words from reading, and make use of them in reading and writing.
W24: To explore opposites.

What you need
● Photocopiable page 94
● a short version of 'The Sword in the Stone'.

Shared text- and word-level work

● Tell the children that King Arthur is one of the greatest characters from the world of myths and legends. Historians agree that such a person probably existed but stories about him have been changed and exaggerated. Elicit from the children that the Arthur stories are legends.
● Tell the story of 'The Sword in the Stone'. Draw attention to the typical story theme of facing a trial. Say that Arthur went on to be a great king of the Court of Camelot, where knights sat at a round table. Discuss the symbolism of the round table.
● Read through 'The Code of Chivalry', which Arthur's knights swore to follow, and establish it as a set of guidelines on how to behave.
● Ask the children to guess the meanings of new vocabulary, and help them with difficult concepts. Discuss each virtue. What word means the opposite of virtue? (Vice.) Identify an opposite of each virtue:

● Prowess/skill – inability	● Faith – despair
● Justice – injustice	● Humility – arrogance
● Loyalty – disloyalty	● Generosity – meanness
● Defence – attack	● Gentleness – roughness.
● Courage – cowardice	

● Point out that the addition of the prefix *in* or *dis* to a word can often provide the word of opposite meaning.
● Note that one of the virtues is *gentleness* and that, although today knights are mainly remembered for their prowess in battle, good knights spent their lives doing good and gentle deeds. Knights fought only to protect people.
● Ask if 'The Code of Chivalry' does or should apply today. How should it be updated (if at all)?

Guided and independent work

● Tell the children that all of Arthur's knights were men, but in this millennium, women have the right to train as knights if they wish to!
● Ask the children to go through the list of virtues and consider what sort of knights they would make. Ask them to tick the virtues they display in their behaviour towards others.

Differentiation

Less able
● Read 'the Code' with the children, considering the meaning of each virtue and asking them to tick the boxes which apply to them.

More able
● Ask children to write out 'the Code', ranking their virtues in order and adding a personal coat of arms.

Plenary

● Tell the children what you believe to be your greatest virtue and why and ask them to say which is theirs. Challenge them to justify this, giving an example.
● Say that with a little work, you believe that all of the children would make great knights, and that a new order of knights is about to be formed called 'Knights of the new millennium'. Tell the children that not only are they going to demonstrate their knightly virtues in school and at home but will also write stories about their adventures, starting in the next lesson!

Objectives

NLS
T8: to write portraits of characters, using story text to describe behaviour and characteristics, and presenting portraits in a variety of ways.
S2: To learn the function of adjectives within sentences.
S3: To use the word *adjective* appropriately.

What you need

● Photocopiable page 94.

Knights of the new millennium

Shared text-level work

● Write the following headings on the board:

> ● Who is in danger?
> ● What is the danger?
> ● What action can be taken?

● Tell the children that they are going to write a modern legend in which they will appear as the hero/heroine. Explain that this will be a dangerous adventure, like ancient legends, but the 'New millennium knight' will save the day!
● Brainstorm a few ideas for each question on the board.
● Tackle the issue of violence. Knights used physical force only as a last resort. Tell the children that the problem in their story must not be solved by fighting but rather ingenuity.
● Ask the children to think about their storyline tonight and then tell their story tomorrow. Say that they can invent a new idea from today's brainstorm. Tell the children that they will eventually write their individual story, but for now, you only want them to think it through as an oral story to be *told*.
● In groups of three, ask one child to write the questions above and record three different answers for each question. Ask the group to decide which is their single best idea and tell this to the class.
● Tell the children that the introduction to their story, will be a description of the main character – the child him/herself!
● What sort of information will the reader want to know about the hero/heroine? Write brief notes on the board:

> ● appearance
> ● where s/he lives
> ● family and friends
> ● hobbies
>
> ● favourite food, books and TV programmes
> ● talents and strongest virtues.

● Tell the children to choose words to describe the character, for example, *brave knight*. Ask what a describing word, like *brave*, is called and elicit *adjective*.
● Begin a shared story on the board, for example:
My name is X and I live in X. I have a secret that only a few friends know. I seem ordinary but actually I am a 'New millennium knight'!

Guided and independent work

● Now ask the children to start drafting their stories with their own character description/introduction.

Plenary

● Ask two volunteers who have completed their introductions to read them out. Discuss the stories' potential for development.

Differentiation

Less able
● Give children the first sentence or two from the shared story to get them started.

More able
● Children should use at least six adjectives in their descriptions. These should be highlighted and then checked by a partner of similar ability for aptness and truth.

UNIT 1 HOUR 8 Narrative: themes

A story worth telling

Objectives

NLS

T7: To describe and sequence key incidents in a variety of ways.
T9: To write a story plan for own myth, fable or traditional story.
W5: To identify mis-spelt words in own writing; to keep individual lists and learn to spell them.
W7: To practise new spellings regularly by 'look, say, cover, write, check' strategy.

What you need

● Photocopiable page 94
● the children's work from Hour 7
● dictionaries
● good-quality paper.

Shared text-level work

● Explain to the children that they are going to publish their special modern legend. They are also going to dedicate the book to someone they love. Discuss the concept of book dedications and tell the children that at the end of this lesson, everyone will name the person or people to whom they are dedicating their books.

● Tell the children that their character descriptions from the last lesson will become the prologue for their story. Explain that a prologue is a type of introduction, giving the reader important information before the story starts, such as setting the scene and introducing the character(s).

Shared word-level work

● Before they rewrite their prologues, ask the children to read them through carefully to check their spellings. Remind them that when self-correcting, they should underline any words they have doubts about and then check these with classmates and/or a dictionary.

Guided and independent work

● Allow ten minutes for self-correction. Tell the children to write three words that were mis-spelled in their spelling jotters. Ask them to add to these the list of virtues from the Code of Chivalry. Let the children know that you will test them on these words on a certain date.

● Ask the children to recall the Look-Say-Cover-Write-Check method of learning spelling, and suggest they use this in spare time in class and for homework.

● Distribute paper and encourage the children to use their best handwriting in rewriting the prologue.

● Gather the children together and ask them if they thought about their stories (from Hour 7) overnight.

● Model the process of storytelling as a way of planning story writing. Ask a child you know will have a good story to tell it to the class.

● Encourage the listeners to make positive comments and to ask the writer questions to help to clarify the storyline. Did the sequence of events make sense? Did the listeners know who everyone was and where they were? Allow five minutes or so for one story and the questions that should follow, and then ask for another volunteer to tell their story and take questions.

● Now ask the children to tell their stories to each other in pairs.

Differentiation

Less able

● Read and correct the children's prologue drafts for them. Listen to every child's story, asking questions to help to develop a coherent narrative.

More able

● Children should add the following words to their spelling list along with definitions from the dictionary: *tournament, opponent, scrupulous.*

Plenary

● Tell the children that tomorrow they will continue to write stories and have one more evening to think about improving the story in the light of the sort of questions that have come up in this session.

● Now ask for the names of people to whom the books are being dedicated and to talk about why they have been chosen, if the children wish to share this.

UNIT 1 HOUR 9 📖 Narrative: themes

Objectives

NLS

T9: To write a story plan for own myth, fable or traditional tale using story themes from reading but substituting different characters or changing the setting.

W25: To practise correct formation of basic joins.

W26: To ensure consistency in size and proportions of letters and the spacing between letters and words.

What you need
- Good-quality paper
- the children's story drafts.

Authors at work

Shared text-level work
- Tell the children that they will now write their stories. Like professional authors, they have established their central character and had time to both think about and share their stories with another person. Tell the children that the story should be written as follows:

> - Title
> - Dedication
> - Prologue
> - Paragraph or Chapter 1 – the problem
> - Paragraph or Chapter 2 – the solution to the problem
> - Paragraph or Chapter 3 – a happy ending and a celebration.

- At this point, explain exactly how the story will be written and depending on time, the ability of the class and the amount of classroom assistant time, select the way forward from the following suggestions:

> - Children write their stories straight on to good paper, in pencil, for you to correct as necessary using an eraser and writing in correct spelling and punctuation.
> - Children write straight onto good paper and you attach Post-it Notes onto the page with correct spellings for children to find and change, using an eraser.
> - Children write a rough copy, you correct and children rewrite onto good paper, incorporating corrections.
> - Children write a rough draft, self- and peer-correct and ask you for a double-check before rewriting.

- It is possible to use a combination of the above methods with different ability groups.
- Remind the children of the importance of beautiful handwriting and give a lesson on the board to reinforce diagonal joins. Also get the children to practise writing letters that are consistent in size. The real purpose of beautiful handwriting and correct spelling and punctuation becomes clear through a publishing project.

Guided and independent work
- Tell the children to work in silence to write their stories, to allow everyone to focus on the task.
- While the children are still writing, carry out a progress check and help those children who:

> - have forgotten their original storyline
> - do not know what to write next
> - do not know how to finish
> - have multiple spelling and punctuation mistakes
> - have gone off task.

Plenary
- Ask some of the children to read their stories to the class.

Differentiation

Less able
- Act as scribe where necessary and correct much of the spelling.

More able
- Children write straight onto good paper. You could attach Post-it Notes onto the page with correct spellings for children to find and change.

UNIT 1 HOUR 10 ▪ Narrative: themes

The new millennium knights

Objectives

NLS
T2: To identify typical story themes, eg good over evil, weak over strong, wise over foolish.
S8: To know other uses of capitalisation from reading, eg names, headings.
W26: To ensure consistency in size and proportion of letters and the spacing between letters and words.

What you need
● Art materials
● final publication materials, depending upon format.

Shared text-level work

● Recap on the children's progress and tell them the order in which to complete remaining tasks – completing the story text, then creating a front cover.

● Ask the children what information will need to be written on the cover. Elicit that there will be a title and the name of the author.

● Suggest to the children that they draw a border around the cover page, using the width of a ruler. Then demonstrate on the board how to place a ruler about one third of the way down the paper and, holding the ruler steady, draw a line along the top and bottom, making parallel lines within which to write the title. Tell the children to touch the top and bottom of these lines with capital letters to ensure consistency in the size of the letters. Explain that the name of the author should be written in lower case further down the cover. Covers should also include an attractive, colourful illustration.

● The book dedication should be written carefully on the inside cover. Demonstrate how to write this in the centre of the page, for example:

> I dedicate this book to
> Mum
> because I love her

● Tell children to choose the most exciting parts of the story to illustrate within the text.

Guided and independent work

● Let the children continue as appropriate. Tell them that, they are working to a publication deadline and will have to focus hard to complete the tasks.

Plenary

● Ask the children to identify the theme of their stories. Although themes may be slightly different, most will fit the general theme of good conquering evil. Ask if any stories were about weak conquering strong, love conquering hate, the wise defeating the foolish. Some children may have more than one theme running through their story.

● Share some of the stories and note that although the details are very different, most share the same theme. Tell children to watch out for these themes used in soap operas, films and novels and to let you know when they recognise them in the future.

● Suggest to the children that they may wish to write sequels to their stories. It could be fun to combine with friends to write stories in which they all feature, rather like *The Three Musketeers* or *X-Men*.

● If possible, arrange a book launch and invite other children and/or parents and carers. Ask for book reviews both within the class and from parents and friends.

Differentiation

Less able
● Children will require a great deal of help in organising and completing tasks.

More able
● Children should read a friend's book and write a blurb for the back cover.

Matilda

Who told Lies, and was Burned to Death

Matilda told such Dreadful Lies,
It made one Gasp and Stretch one's Eyes;
Her Aunt, who, from her Earliest Youth,
Had kept a Strict Regard for Truth,
Attempted to Believe Matilda:
The effort very nearly killed her,
And would have done so, had not She
Discovered this Infirmity.
For once, towards the Close of Day,
Matilda, growing tired of play,
And finding she was left alone,
Went tiptoe to the Telephone
And summoned the Immediate Aid
Of London's Noble Fire-Brigade.
Within an hour the Gallant Band
Were pouring in on every hand,
From Putney, Hackney Downs, and Bow,
With Courage high and Hearts a-glow
They galloped, roaring through the Town,
'Matilda's House is Burning Down!'
Inspired by British Cheers and Loud
Proceeding from the Frenzied Crowd,
They ran their ladders through a score
Of windows on the Ball Room Floor;
And took Peculiar Pains to Souse
The Pictures up and down the House,

Until Matilda's Aunt succeeded
In showing them they were not needed,
And even then she had to pay
To get the Men to go away!
It happened that a few Weeks later
Her Aunt was off to the Theatre
To see that Interesting Play
The Second Mrs Tanqueray.
She had refused to take her Niece
To hear this Entertaining Piece:
A deprivation Just and Wise
To Punish her for Telling Lies.
That Night a Fire *did* break out-
You should have heard Matilda Shout!
You should have heard her Scream and Bawl,
And throw the window up and call
To People passing in the Street –
(The rapidly increasing Heat
Encouraging her to obtain
Their confidence)-but all in vain!
For every time She shouted 'Fire!'
They only answered 'Little liar!'
And therefore when her Aunt returned,
Matilda, and the House, were Burned.

Hilaire Belloc

TERM 2

George and the Dragon

The people of Joppa, next to the Mediterranean sea, were in despair because a terrible dragon was attacking and eating people and even the bravest soldier was too frightened to fight the dragon.

The people agreed on a plan. Every week, the name of one of the people was pulled out in a draw and that person was tied to a steak outside the town and left for the dragon to devour. The family of the sacrificed person was given a great deal of money in recognition of the good deed they had done for the town.

The dragon was pleased with the arrangement, particularly when he saw that the kindest and most beautiful woman in Joppa was tied to the steak to be his next victim.

Just then, George, a Christian knight in armour, came riding by on his way home from the crusades. Seeing what was about to happen, he drew out his sword and rode at the dragon. There was a terrible fight, with fire, roaring and a lot of blood but George managed to slay the dragon and set the beautiful woman free.

There was a great celebration and later, George married the woman. The people of Joppa became Christians because of George.

M SCHOLASTIC

Beowulf and Grendel

The Danish people were in despair because the terrible and hideous monster, Grendel, was killing their best warriors. Grendel lived in a cave beneath the sea, but at night, he would sneak in to the Great Hall of the Danes' castle and pounce on them as they slept.

Beowulf was the great warrior of the Geat people and he came to Denmark with his men to help with their dreadful plight. At night, Beowulf stayed awake and even he was terrified when he saw the terrible monster sliding through the darkness.

But brave Beowulf fought Grendel. Grendel managed to escape but as he twisted and tore himself away from Beowulf's grasp, Beowulf ripped off one of the monster's huge legs!

The following night Grendel's mother, who was even more terrifying than her son, came to take her revenge. There was another ferocious fight and the noise frightened people so much that they ran away, leaving Beowulf alone to deal with the monster. Beowulf was determined to finish off the two monsters and followed Grendel's mother back to her cave. He was exhausted, but he saw a huge sword and with this he slew both monsters. The metal of the sword dissolved in the blood of the monsters and Beowulf was left with only the hilt.

When the Danes heard the great news there was a huge party and although the Danes were never too keen on the Geats, they had to admit that Beowulf was the greatest hero ever!

The Code of Chivalry

Prowess
Try to be excellent in everything you do. Use your strength to help others rather than yourself.

Justice
Always try to do the right thing, not just what suits you.

Loyalty
Always support the people you love. Don't let people down.

Defence
Always be ready to defend the people who depend upon you and also the people you think deserve defending.

Courage
Being a knight means following the hardest path. Learn that you have to stand by the truth at all times even if it is easier to lie.

Faith
Have faith in your beliefs. This will give you hope when the terrible things that other people do make you want to despair.

Humility
Praise the good things that others do. Do not boast about yourself.

Generosity
Be as generous as you are able. Don't be greedy.

Gentleness
Always strive to do the knightly thing even if you realise you will never do it perfectly. Trying your best makes you a better person. Always be gentle and considerate to others.

UNIT 2

Narrative: plot

This unit makes the most of children's love of fairy stories. There is critical thinking involved in analysing plot and structure and in interpretation. Children are challenged to extend stories into sequels and to adapt stories to modern settings. Through these activities, children perceive the similarities of theme and plot in many stories. The particular language style used in fairy stories is a defining feature of the genre and it is only through reading and hearing a wealth of stories and telling stories to others that children will thoroughly grasp this language.

This unit suggests the creation of a fairy tale world in the classroom. Art lessons could be focused to create dazzling displays of witches and castles, princesses and heroes on horseback. Use drama to develop storytelling skills. Opportunities to debate moral issues are raised by traditional tales, linking to PSHE and citizenship

Hour	Shared text-level work	Shared word-/ sentence-level work	Guided and independent work	Plenary
1 What is a fairy story?	Identifying common features of favourite fairy tales.	Practising endings for plural nouns.	Choosing first and last lines from fairy tales.	Seeing language similarities in chosen sentences; thinking about how to split chosen stories.
2 Telling a fairy story	Generating criteria for good storytelling.		Dividing the story and creating story prompts in notes and pictures; performing to other groups.	Discussing how helpful the prompts were; taking feedback.
3 Fairy tale sequels	Establishing what goes into a sequel.		Brainstorming ideas for sequel to group story; telling sequel to other groups; writing sequels, checking spellings in a dictionary.	Sharing finished stories.
4 The main events	Establishing sequence of events in *Cinderella*.		Using different methods of sequencing a fairy story.	Comparing different presentation methods.
5 Modern-day Snow White	Discussing themes of *Snow White*, relating this to fairy tale genre.		Planning story plot for modernised *Snow White*.	Sharing stories so far; telling stories to other classes; bringing to publication.

Key assessment opportunities
● Can the children work together to retell a fairy tale for infants?
● Can they transfer a fairy tale plot to modern times?
● Can they identify main points in a story?

What is a fairy story?

Objectives

NLS
T1: To investigate the styles and voices of traditional story language.
T2: To identify typical story themes.
S4: To extend knowledge and understanding of pluralisation.
W9: To investigate and identify basic rules for changing the spelling of nouns when s is added.

What you need
● A variety of fairy stories.

Shared text-level work
● Write the children's favourite fairy story titles on the board, including any they found frightening when they were younger.
● Discuss some of the common features of fairy tale books, such as beautiful illustrations and elicit typical story features:

- ● magic
- ● recognisable character types - giants, fairies, witches, princes, princesses,
- ● settings like forests and woods in lands far, far away
- ● dwellings that are either humble or regal (cottages and palaces)
- ● beginnings such as *Once upon a time* or *Long, long ago*
- ● 'baddies' that are defeated and 'goodies' that all live happily ever after!

● Continue this discussion of commonalities to include themes:

- ● good over evil
- ● the transforming power of love
- ● the seemingly ordinary being extraordinary.

Shared word- and sentence-level work
● When talking about characters, discuss that the characters often come in groups. Write the following on the board:

- ● an ugly sister
- ● one little pig
- ● one dwarf
- ● a fairy.

● Ask the children to write the plurals of these characters.
● Explain the rule for changing nouns into plurals by adding s, as in *sisters* and *pigs*. However, when a noun ends in *f*, we drop the *f* and add *ves* (*dwarves*). Nouns ending in *y* drop the *y* and add *ies* (*fairies*).
● Check the children's answers to see who remembered this rule.

Guided and independent work
● Distribute strips of paper and several fairy stories to each group of four. Tell them to look through the stories and copy first and final sentences. These will be displayed so must be carefully spelled, punctuated, and written.
● Tell the groups to choose a story that they all like and that can be split into four parts for storytelling to a younger class. Avoid *Snow White* and *Cinderella* as these will be studied in future lessons.

Differentiation

Less able
● Tell children to complete only the first two examples of singular to plural.

More able
● Ask the children to write the plurals for: Hunter's knife, Babe in the wood, Genie in the bottle.

Plenary
● Ask the children to read out one closing or opening sentence. Discuss the language similarities before displaying for reference.
● Now ask the groups to name their chosen story and explain how it is to be split for retelling. Advise everyone to think about their part of the story before going to sleep at night.

UNIT 2 HOUR 2 ▢ Narrative: plot

Telling a fairy story

● Before the session, organise either for groups to go to another class or for another class to come visit the storytellers.
● Ask the children to suggest criteria for good storytelling. List them on the board, for example:

> ● Give the title of the story.
> ● Speak clearly and not too quickly.
> ● Vary the volume.
> ● Vary the pace (guided by meaning and punctuation).
> ● Put expression into the voice in order to convey meaning and characterisation.
> ● Keep the listeners' attention by using facial expressions and gestures.
> ● Use different voices for different characters' speech in dialogue.
> ● Stand or sit still.
> ● Don't leave gaps between the sections – keep the story seamless.

● Tell them to take these points into consideration when rehearsing their stories.

Guided and independent work
● Tell the children that as part of the preparation for telling their chosen fairy story, you want them to draw a small picture illustrating the main event in the section of the story for which they have responsibility.
● Organise the groups and ask them to re-establish story parts, discuss the main events and draw their pictures on the top half of A4 sheets.
● Now explain that story continuity will only be guaranteed if every group member knows exactly when his or her part of the story begins and ends. Tell the children to rehearse the storytelling, stopping to allow each group member to make notes in the bottom half of their A4 sheet, as a reminder of when to start and stop. This note may be the last sentence spoken or the last main event described by each story teller. These notes, together with the picture will form a story prompt. Stress to the children to keep to notes as they are going to *tell* the story not *read* it.
● Tell the children that following the storytelling sessions, the pictures and the prompt notes will be displayed to show organisation of the stories. It will be interesting to compare how different groups who have chosen the same story have decided to divide the story.
● Allow extra time for rehearsal and note-making before pairing the groups and letting them perform for one another. Tell them to take a few minutes after each performance for comments and advice.

Plenary
● Discuss the usefulness of the story prompts in ensuring continuity. Some children find prompts useful and others find them distracting. Display prompt sheets together for each story.
● Get feedback from the audiences to share with the storytellers.

UNIT 2 HOUR 3 📃 Narrative: plot

Fairy tale sequels

Objectives

NLS

T6: To plan main points as a structure for story writing, considering how to capture points in a few words that can be elaborated later.
T10: To write alternative sequels to traditional stories.
W5: To identify mis-spelt words in own writing.
W19: To use dictionaries to learn or check the spellings of words.
W22: To know the quartiles of the dictionary.

What you need

● Dictionaries.

Shared text-level work

● Many of the children will be Harry Potter fans and will understand the term *sequel*. Discuss that a sequel usually includes the same main characters, setting and style as the original story. The characters have a new problem and this has to be solved by the end of the sequel. Use *Cinderella* as an example:

> When Prince Charming and Cinderella returned from their honeymoon, the palace gates were locked and a big sign said, 'Keep out. Property of the ugly sisters.'
>
> Before going on her honeymoon, Cinderella had made the mistake of forgiving her step sisters and allowing them to move into the palace to share her good fortune!

● Ask the children what they think will happen next. Take different ideas, working through each one quickly to a conclusion.

Guided and independent work

● In their storytelling groups, ask the children to brainstorm problems that might occur at the beginning of a sequel and then note how the story will develop. Remind them that even if the villain in their original story seemed to have been killed, in a fairy story, baddies can always magically be brought back to life to cause more trouble in the sequel!
● Tell the children to use first and last sentences displayed on the wall (or variations of them), to help to ensure that their stories are told in fairy story language.
● Allow about five minutes for this task, and then pair the groups as before, telling the children to share the bare bones of the sequel with the other group.
● When they retell the story to an audience, children often realise as they speak that some parts of the story do not make sense and they self-correct as they go along. Encourage the other group to make comments to reinforce ideas or offer suggestions for improvements.
● Now ask the children to write their sequels individually. Allow twenty minutes for this and, whatever stage they have reached in writing, children should stop and read their work, underlining possible spelling mistakes and checking that the story makes sense.
● Practise identifying the quartiles of the dictionary and let the children check and correct their spellings.

Differentiation

Less able
● Children should write the first and last sentences of the story using language of fairy tales displayed on the wall.

More able
● Children should write blurb for their story to be displayed on the wall.

Plenary

● Ask the children who have completed stories to read these out to the class. Praise their efforts and encourage analytical comments from members of the audience.
● Polished copies of the sequels should be completed for homework and displayed with the prompt notes of the original stories.
● Arrange for the children to rehearse and then share the story with the Key Stage 1 audiences.

The main events

Objectives

NLS
T6: To plan main points, considering how to capture points in a few words.
T7: To describe and sequence key incidents in a variety of ways, eg by listing, making simple storyboards.

Shared text-level work

● Develop the idea that if we know the main points of any story, it is possible to retell the story. Recall the story of *Cinderella*, writing the sequence on the board:

1. Cinderella cleans and cooks for her nasty stepsisters.
2. The Prince invites the family to a ball but Cinderella cannot go.
3. Cinderella's godmother dresses her beautifully and sends her to the ball, warning her that she must be home before midnight.
4. Cinderella and the Prince dance and fall in love.
5. Cinderella runs from the ball as the clock strikes, losing her shoe.
6. The Prince tries the shoe on every maiden in the land to find his love. It fits Cinderella.
7. The Prince and Cinderella get married, to the dismay of the stepsisters!

● List on the board the following methods of charting the main points in a story, and discuss them:

● A sequence of sentences with bullet points or numbers.
● A sequence of storyboards with line drawings and short captions.
● A flow chart with short sentences in boxes, with arrows joining the boxes.
● A zig-zag book, with main incidents illustrated and captioned, rather like a cartoon strip.

Guided and independent work

● Organise groups of four (or five if you want to treat bullet points and numbering separately) and tell the children to divide the tasks above for *Cinderella* or another story, with one child in each group drawing or writing the main points in one of the ways shown on the board. Note group discussion, fairness, agreement and compromise. Explain that when easier/quicker tasks are completed, it is every group member's responsibility to assist the others in completing unfinished tasks. Tell the children that finished work will be displayed for peer evaluation and your assessment.
● Written statements may be taken from the list on the board and the pictures should represent the statements.
● Tell the children to check their spelling and punctuation and then read each other's work to check for sense and coherence. They should also check that all the agreed main events are included.

Differentiation

Less able
● Allocate the task of sequencing using bullet points.

More able
● Organise more able children into a group and challenge them to work on a different story (not *Snow White* or *Cinderella*).

Plenary

● More able children who tackled a new fairy story should report on the main events they identified. Ask the rest of the class if they agree with their choices.
● Compare the different ways of presenting the same story. Which do they find easiest/most interesting to follow as a reader? Which did they enjoy producing?
● Discuss what is missing from these stories: description of setting, characterisation and so on.

UNIT 2 HOUR 5 ◻ Narrative: plot

Modern-day Snow White

Objectives

NLS

T2: To identify typical story themes.
T9: To write a story plan for own myth, fable or traditional tale using story theme from reading but substituting different characters or changing the setting.

S&L

31 Group discussion and interaction: To actively include and respond to all members of the group.

What you need
● Simple version of *Snow White*
● photocopiable page 101.

Shared text-level work
● Read or tell a short version of the *Snow White* story. Check that the children are clear about the main characters and events.
● Explain that all stories have a plot, which is the storyline. Recap that stories also have a theme, which is the underlying message of the story and brainstorm some of these (from Hour 1 and Unit 1).
● Ask which of the themes runs through *Snow White*. (Love/goodness overcoming evil/wickedness.) Ask how this is represented explicitly in the story. (The Prince's loving kiss is the antidote to the Queen's poisoned apple.)
● Tell the children that it is possible to keep the same theme and similar characters and transfer a traditional tale to a modern setting. Snow White, for example, could live in the nearest town. What modern name could she have? The wicked Queen could still be the girl's aunt, but not a queen! What clothes would Snow White wear? Instead of trying to kill the girl with a poisoned apple, perhaps her aunt could set fire to the house and Snow White could be saved by a handsome fire-fighter! Offer suggestions in order to encourage the children to think in this new way. Could the Seven Dwarves be a pop boy band who share a house or flat in town? Once the brainstorm is running, give children the opportunity to comment on one another's ideas. Stress the fact that the final story must be coherent.

Guided and independent work
● Read through photocopiable page 101. Organise the children into groups to work through the sheet together. By discussing and answering the questions, the children will plan a story plot.
● Then tell the groups to use the notes to create a skeleton plot for a modern-day 'Snow White' story. Remind them to make up a new title. Stress that you will be visiting groups as they work to ensure they are all contributing ideas, listening to each other and discussing fairly.
● Once they have agreed on the bare bones, ask them to split the story into parts for storytelling as a group. Suggest that they make and use story prompts only if they were useful last time.

Plenary
● Ask each group to tell their story, and encourage comments on good points from the rest of the class and points for improvement if appropriate.
● Note that the theme has remained consistent through several different versions of the story.
● If possible, arrange for amendments, rehearsals and a storytelling session with a younger class.
● Encourage children to write up and illustrate their stories.

Differentiation

Less able
● Ask children to design a poster advertising the modern fairytale.

More able
● Encourage more able children to publish the story using ICT.

A modern Snow White story

1. Where does Snow White live?

2. Who is the character that is trying to kill her?

3. Why does this character hate Snow White?

4. In the traditional tale, the wicked Queen sent the woodsman to kill Snow White. Who might this 'assassin' be in a modern story?

5. Snow White finds a house with a door open and nobody in. Where might this building be?

6. Who are 'The Seven Dwarves'?

7. The 'Prince', who saves Snow White might be a firefighter, police officer or doctor. You may be able to think of a better idea. Who is he?

8. A magic mirror won't tell the evil character where Snow White is, so how does she find out?

9. When she finds Snow White how does she try to kill her?

10. How does the character who loves Snow White save her?

11. What happens at the end of your modern story?

12. What is Snow White's modern name?

UNIT 3

Poetry

The ability of children to understand complex concepts about poetry should not be underestimated. The best way to develop critical thinking is to encourage questioning and discussion rather than 'give answers'. In performing poetry, children learn the crucial importance of punctuation and rhythm. Decisions are made about pace, volume, tone and expression. When assessing the performance of others, children are at the same time reflecting upon their own interpretation and delivery.

Teaching this unit should be fun! It is important for children to understand the poems but the critical thinking sessions should be carried out at a brisk pace. It is important to provide performers with an audience and the idea of a poetry event at the end of the unit will give real purpose to the work. The event could be anything from inviting another class through to a full scale afternoon/evening concert.

Active, auditory and social learners will thrive on the activities in this unit. Shy children are supported in structured collaborative tasks. There are opportunities for dynamic social learning, when children take poetry to the people as playground poets and hit-and-run poets!

Hour	Shared text-level work	Shared word-/ sentence-level work	Guided and independent work	Plenary
1 The poet's voice	Reading 'The Tide Rises, The Tide Falls' and discussing meaning; considering performance features.	Looking at words with silent letters.	Rehearsing and performing verses of the poem in groups, using annotations; making improvements after audience comments.	Organising sets to perform the entire poem.
2 Using different voices	Discussing enjoyment of books and poetry; reading 'Forbidden Poem' and talking about meaning.		Selecting poems that have affected them; practising performance of 'Forbidden Poem'.	Recording class performance; setting up a life-changing poetry collection box.
3 Language detectives	Discussing dialects and accents; reading 'Wha Me Mudder Do' and 'Owl of the Greenwood'; choral performance.	Inferring meaning from context; using grammar/ parts of speech to guess at meanings.	Analysing one verse at a time; experimenting with performances.	Examples of interesting performance and comments upon interpretation.
4 Playground poets	Reading 'Swing, Swing'; establishing meaning and the use and effects of metaphor, simile and alliteration.	Revising the importance of punctuation to the meaning of poetry.	Interpreting the poem; reciting as a chorus; writing verses in the playground.	Letting hit-and-run poets loose on willing volunteers!
5 What-ifs	Discussing meaning of 'The Worries'; closely studying beats in the couplets; composing couplets as a class.		Writing own 'What if' couplets.	Recital of poem with new lines inserted.

Key assessment opportunities
● Can the children interpret and recite poetry with meaning?
● Can they comment analytically on peer performance?
● Do they appreciate the importance of reading and writing appropriate punctuation in poetry?

The poet's voice

Shared text-level work
● Tell the children that in this unit they will be preparing for a poetry performance and choosing and collecting poems.
● Explain that in reciting poetry the performers communicate the meaning of the poem to the audience. It is important therefore to understand and interpret the messages in the poem.
● Display and read 'The Tide Rises, The Tide Falls'. Then ask the children to re-read it by themselves and think silently about the meaning for a few minutes.
● Ask if anyone has questions about the poem and note these on the board. What happens to the traveller? Ask what the poet is telling us (the enduring, continuing nature of the sea and its disinterest in others) before asking for opinions about favourite lines.
● Now discuss the questions on the board. As far as possible, lead children to answer these questions themselves.
● Tell the children that they are going to prepare a recital of one verse of the poem. Discuss the following factors that groups will have to consider in their performance:

● the importance of reading the punctuation
● the rhythm or the beat
● volume
● pace
● expression.

● Display the list for reference throughout the unit.

Shared word-level work
● Write the word *neigh* on the board and ask how it is said. Explain that *eigh* forms an *ay* sound and that the *g* is silent. Ask for other examples of words in which letters are silent (these are often easier to identify at the start): *gnaw, know, knee, gnat, castle* and so on.

Guided and independent work
● Organise six mixed-ability groups. Name two groups A, two groups B and two groups C. Tell groups A to prepare verse 1 for performance, groups B to prepare verse 2 and groups C to prepare verse 3.
● Ask the groups to discuss how the lines should be performed. Tell them to refer to the points on the wall annotate the poem to remind them of their decisions. Allow ten minutes for rehearsals.
● Watch each group's performance in turn. Encourage comments from the audience, using the list on display to focus responses. Give another five minutes for making changes in the light of comments.

Plenary
● Identify a set of ABC groups to perform the entire poem together, each group reciting only their own verse. The other set will also perform the whole poem.

Using different voices

Objectives

NLS

T4: To choose and prepare poems for performance, identifying appropriate expression, tone, volume and use of voices and other sounds.
T5: To improve performance, taking note of punctuation and meaning.

What you need
● Photocopiable pages 109 and 110
● poetry anthologies
● box file
● video recorder.

Shared text-level work
● Read 'Forbidden Poem'. Discuss the idea of 'getting lost' in a book and elicit common expressions on this, for example, being *immersed in a book* or *getting into a book* and the noun *book worm* to describe someone engrossed in books.
● Explain that the poet has taken this idea literally and created a place in which poetry lives and into which a person can enter. Ask the children to describe the trap door and to tell you what is written on the door.
● What does the poet mean when he says that a child will never be the same once having read a poem? Discuss that discovering poetry can be a joy; a poem can reinforce ideas a person already believes, change them completely or lead a person to see the world in a different way.
● Ask the children how poetry has changed or reinforced their ideas and add your own examples. For example, what do they understand about nature after reading 'The Tide Rises, The Tide Falls'?
● In the last verse of 'Forbidden Poem', the child becomes 'trapped' in the world of thoughts and questions about the meaning of our lives. Discuss if it is a bad thing to be trapped in the world of poetry!

Guided and independent work
● Distribute personal anthologies or poetry books and ask the children to spend ten minutes on their own, identifying one or two lines of poetry that have changed them in some way, for example:

● making them laugh
● making them see something in a new way
● frightening them
● introducing them to a new idea
● enabling them to understand that the poet agrees with something they have already thought.

● Ask the children to copy these lines onto strips of paper and collect them in a box file.
● Organise the class into six groups and distribute one copy of photocopiable page 110 to every group. Remind the children of their oral poetry work from Hour 1 and read verse 1 as a class. Allocate the next six verses between the groups and ask the children to discuss and rehearse their verse, using volume and expression as suggested.

Differentiation

Less able
● Children will need help in selecting significant lines of poetry. Read one funny or sad poem, discuss it and allow a choice of lines.

More able
● Children should explain the idea of the 'Forbidden poetry box' to teachers and ask for contributions.
● Encourage them to add their own notes to photocopiable page 110.

Plenary
● Record the class saying the poem, with first and last verses performed together. Replay the performance and invite comments for improvements. Allow another brief rehearsal, then record a final performance to be shown on parents evening or taken home to share with parents.
● Make the box file of life-changing poetry available for sharing. Encourage parents and friends to contribute extracts to the 'Forbidden poetry box'.

Language detectives

Objectives

NLS
T4: To prepare poems for performance, identifying appropriate expression, tone, volume and use of voices.
T5: To rehearse and improve performance, taking note of punctuation and meaning.
S1: To use awareness of grammar to decipher new or unfamiliar words.
W18: To infer the meaning of unknown words from context.

S&L
29 Speaking: To prepare poems for performance.

What you need
● Photocopiable pages 111 and 112.

Shared work
● Before reading 'Wha Me Mudder Do', explain that the poem describes a particular culture and is in a form of English developed outside Britain.
● Refer to the very diverse ways in which English is spoken in Wales and Scotland and around England, for example, the West Country and the North-East. Establish an ethos of respect and appreciation for others people's accents and ways of speaking.
● Read and enjoy the poem, enunciating clearly and emphasising the fast pace and clear rhythm.
● Challenge the children to be language detectives, inferring meaning from context and grammar. For example, *mudder* must be a noun as it is clearly something or someone belonging to *me*. Write *mek*, *plantain* and *fufu* on the board and ask the children to try and guess the meanings of these words.
● Discuss some of the critical thinking points raised in the annotations.
● Next, rehearse a performance of the poem. Practise the chorus as a whole class and then assign the other lines to be said individually by able performers. Allow children a few minutes to decide with what expression, volume, pace and rhythm they will say their particular line.
● Perform the poem a couple of times to ensure that every child participates.
● Now read 'Owl of the Greenwood'. Re-read the chorus together, helping the children to appreciate the onomatopoeia and the sound of the owl, and the punctuation.

Guided and independent work
● Organise mixed-ability groups of four and divide the three verses among the groups, ensuring that each group has only one verse to concentrate on.
● Encourage the children to spend a few minutes talking about the meaning of their verse, then allocating the lines among themselves so that every child has responsibility for saying one line in each verse. There are only three lines in verse one and therefore one person in this group should say the title and the name of the poet.
● Tell the children to take time to discuss, practise and experiment with ways to say their lines. After each verse the whole group should recite the chorus together. Observe and note groups that are developing an interesting presentation.
● After an appropriate time ask groups to change verses and start again. Try to ensure each group explores all three verses.

Differentiation

Less able
● Children should rehearse their line with you before performance.

More able
● The group identified by the class as best performers should recite the poem at an assembly.

Plenary
● Choose one or two groups to perform each verse for the class and invite comments about interpretation. Ask the children to choose a group that they felt had interpreted the poem well and had communicated the spirit of what the poet was saying in her poem.

UNIT 3 HOUR 4 ■ Poetry

What you need
- Photocopiable pages 108-113
- camcorder
- chalk.

Playground poets

Shared text-level work
- Display and read 'Swing, Swing', emphasising the swinging, lilting rhythm, which carries the poem along at a cracking pace. Express the theme of freedom, and slow down at the end.
- Establish the children's understanding of the poem and include consideration of metaphor, simile, alliteration and use of punctuation.

Guided and independent work
- Tell the children that the 'wholeness' of this poem is important, as meaning flows and moves dynamically from verse to verse, so they will have to work carefully to generate a coherent group reading.
- Organise four groups to interpret and perform one verse each. Go around the room to hear the groups' discussions of content and rehearsals of interpretation.
- Ask each group to perform and encourage the other groups to comment upon good points. How coherently will the different verses join together? Spend a few minutes sharing ideas for improvements.
- Let the groups have another short rehearsal to incorporate these changes, then gather the class together for a recital of the whole poem.
- Record the performance for critical comment afterwards, when preparing the poetry event.
- Now distribute playground chalk and tell the children that they are going to become playground poets, sharing their poetry with the rest of the school. There are two ways of doing this activity:

> - Allow every child to choose their favourite verse from any of the poems studied and ask them to copy this on the ground in the school playing area. Underneath the verse, they should add the caption *If you want to know more about this poem please see [name of child]*.
> - Organise poem groups, according to the children's choice of favourite poem, with one child responsible for writing one verse. Verses should be numbered and each poem written horizontally across the ground so that all the children can be writing at the same time.

- Remind the children that poets use punctuation marks carefully to help the reader understand and enjoy the poem. It would be insulting to these poets to miss out punctuation or to include the wrong marks! Spelling and handwriting are also very important because there is no point in writing text in the playground that others cannot read.

Plenary
- Now tell the children they are hit-and-run poets. Quickly take the class to an area of the school where there is an informal audience and present a class reading or recital of 'Swing, Swing'. Visit, for example, the headteacher, office staff, lunchtime supervisors, caretaker, parents waiting to collect children before the bell, or any other people who will cooperate in listening to the children.

Differentiation

Less able
- Children should be supervised and given help in writing their verse of poetry in the playground.

More able
- Encourage children to select and write longer and more complex poetry in the playground, perhaps even their own compositions.

What-ifs

Objectives

NLS

T11: To write new or extended verses for performance based on models of performance and oral poetry read, eg rhythms, repetition.

What you need
● Photocopiable page 114.

Shared text-level work
● Display and read the very simple poem 'The Worries' with an emphasis on the beat and the desperation in expression.
● Children will identify with the theme of this poem and there should be lively discussion!
● Go through the couplets one at a time, noting that some of the lines describe serious, important fears: *What if I did not try my best?* And other lines are comical and absurd: *What if I shrink to the size of a pea?*
● Talk about typical night-time fears, keeping the subject light. Ask everyone to identify one fear that can keep them awake or has kept them awake in the past.
● Tell the children that they are going to use this fear as the subject of a rhyming couplet for inclusion in a class poem about 'What-ifs'.
● Stress that everyone needs to use the same rhythm. Clap the beat of lines 5 and 6 and 7 and 8, as these have a regular beat (of six beats, then eight). Point out that two beats in each line have been used up with the words *What if*. This means that new words in the first line must fit four beats and the second line must fit six beats.
● Remind them of syllables in words by going round the class clapping the syllables in people's names.
● Children may observe that the poet breaks his beat pattern later in the poem, but tell them that, as less experienced poets, they will be sticking to the regular number of beats.
● Try out a few new couplets as a class, encouraging the children to attempt rhyme as well as rhythm.

Guided and independent work
● Ask the children to work out their what-if rhyming couplets. Ask the children to share these with partners to check for sense and the correct beat. Share some examples with the class.
● Distribute horizontal strips of A3 paper and ask the children to write their lines on this. Children who have not succeeded in creating a couplet should copy one from the board or one from John Foster's poem.

Plenary
● To present the poem, ask the whole class to recite the first four lines together and the last two lines of 'The Worries'. In between the beginning and the end, assign places for individuals to say their lines in the poem.
● If you decide to use this poem as part of the poetry event, you will need to choose the best lines to make up the middle of the poem when the rest of the class recite the beginning and end.
● Display all of the children's couplets.

Differentiation

Less able
● Let children use an example from the board, changing one or two words.

More able
● Ask children to write more than one couplet, then go on to help other children.

The Tide Rises, The Tide Falls

The tide rises, the tide falls,
The twilight darkens, the curlew calls;
Along the sea-sands damp and brown
The traveller hastens toward the town;
   And the tide rises, the tide falls.

Darkness settles on roofs and walls,
But the sea in the darkness calls and calls;
The little waves, with their soft white hands,
Efface the footprints in the sands,
   And the tide rises, the tide falls.

The morning breaks; the steeds in their stalls
Stamp and neigh, as the hostler calls;
The day returns; but nevermore
Returns the traveller to the shore,
   And the tide rises, the tide falls.

Henry Wadsworth Longfellow

Unifying rhyme scheme
Insistent but indifferent

Careless wiping out of human evidence
Consistent personification/ anthropomorphisation
Alliteration and repetition to emphasise movement and power

Elemental, impatient
Who is the hostler?
What has happened to the traveller?
Sea continues its way, regardless

Forbidden Poem

This poem is not for children
Keep out!
There is a big oak door
in front of this poem.
It's locked.
And on the door is a notice
in big red letters.
It says: Any child who enters here
will never be the same again.
WARNING. KEEP OUT.

But what's this?
A key in the keyhole.
And what's more,
nobody's about.

"Go on. Look,"
says a little voice
inside your head.
"Surely a poem
cannot strike you dead?"

You turn the key.
The door swings wide.
And then you witness
what's inside.

And from that day
you'll try in vain.
You'll never be the same again.

Tony Mitton

The poetry is a metaphor

First two verses are in blank verse

The first may be a challenge to children who would not normally be interested in poetry. The second is an invitation to do something they really should not, to tempt children into the world of ideas.

The first two stanzas set the scene.

In the third, we find the beginnings of simple rhyme becoming more regular in the fourth and fifth.

The rhyme scheme creates an atmosphere of confusion and disorganisation – perhaps reflective of the thought processes of children who find it hard to concentrate. of the last verse.

TERM 2

Performing poetry

Type of voice to try	Forbidden Poem	Your own ideas
[VERSE 1] A clear, definite voice as if giving an order – bossy!	This poem is not for children Keep out! There is a big oak door in front of this poem. It's locked. And on the door is a notice in big red letters. It says: Any child who enters here will never be the same again. WARNING. KEEP OUT.	
[VERSE 2] A sneaky, whispering voice	But what's this? A key in the keyhole. And what's more, nobody's about.	
[VERSE 3] A commanding voice, becoming sneering in the last line.	"Go on. Look," says a little voice inside your head. "Surely a poem cannot strike you dead?"	
[VERSE 4] Quietly; scared, worried	You turn the key. The door swings wide. And then you witness what's inside.	
[VERSE 5] Confident, definite	And from that day you'll try in vain. You'll never be the same again. *Tony Mitton*	

■SCHOLASTIC

Wha Me Mudder Do

Mek me tell you wha me Mudder do
wha me mudder do
wha me mudder do

Me mudder pound plantain mek fufu
Me mudder catch crab mek calaloo stew

Mek me tell you wha me mudder do
wha me mudder do
wha me mudder do

Me mudder beat hammer
Me mudder turn screw
she paint chair red
then she paint it blue

Mek me tell you wha me mudder do
wha me mudder do
wha me mudder do

Me mudder chase bad-cow
with one 'Shoo'
she paddle down river
in she own canoe
Ain't have nothing
dat me mudder can't do
Ain't have nothing
dat me mudder can't do

Mek me tell you

Grace Nichols

Skilful structure – appears primitive and repetitive yet conveys the excitement of a sleeve-tugging proud child

Varied tasks; some traditionally associated with mothers, some more associated with fathers

Repetition adds to the sense of frantic enthusiasm

Patois in which English expressions have been altered

Rhyming scheme almost wholly consisting of the sound oo which moves the poem along at a swift pace

Her own canoe – status

TERM 2

Owl of the Greenwood

'Owl
Who?
Who are you?
Who?'
    'I am owl,
    night's eyes,
    wise beyond understanding.'
'Who?
Who are you?
Who?'
    'I am owl,
    shadow of shadows,
    owner of forests,
    beautiful beyond comprehension.'
'Who?
Who are you?
Who?'
    'I am owl,
    plucker of moonbeams;
    owl, most mysterious.
    Beware.'

Patricia Hubbell

Chorus/refrain

Represents the sound of the owl's call and also insistently asks the question

The poet has subtly changed the received truth that owls can see at night

Makes the reader wonder what night would see and makes us feel scared

Stature and importance of the owl increases

With what feelings do we associate forests and shadows?

What is the effect of this claim?

In what sense could the owl be said to be the 'owner'?

Is this metaphor a musical reference or of power and ownership?

Supernatural powers make the one word final line even more powerful

Atmosphere of danger and mystery

Swing, Swing

Swing, swing,
Sing, sing,
Here! my throne and I am a king!
Swing, sing,
Swing, sing,
Farewell, earth, for I'm on the wing!

Low, high,
Here I fly,
Like a bird through sunny sky;
Free, free,
Over the lea,
Over the mountain, over the sea!

Soon, soon,
Afternoon,
Over the sunset, over the moon;
Far, far,
Over all bar,
Sweeping on from star to star!

No, no,
Low, low,
Sweeping daisies with my toe.
Slow, slow,
To and fro,
Slow — slow — slow — slow.

William Allingham

Swinging, swaying, lilting rhythm

Repetition like the back and forth of a swing

Metaphor speaks of child's sense of power and exhilaration

Should be recited with bravado

Simile

Vocabulary emphasises sense of motion, openness and freedom

'Lea' is a poetic word meaning 'field'

Repetition indicates how time flies when you're enjoying yourself!

This verse emphasises the freedom afforded by this experience

There is a build up from verse one with take off, to verse two over mountains and sea, to verse three beyond the stars

He is reluctant to stop

He's back to earth

Pace and rhythm slows, the exhilaration is passed and things come to a halt

The Worries

At night-time, as I lie in bed,
The Worries swirl around my head:

What if I'm late for school?
What if I blush and feel a fool?

What if I fail the test?
What if I did not try my best?

What if they call me names?
What if I can't join in their games?

What if my report's bad?
What if my Dad gets very mad?

What if Mum and Dad break up?
What if Mum finds I've used her make-up?

What if aliens kidnap me?
What if I shrink to the size of a pea?

What if I'm attacked by a shark?
What if I start to glow in the dark?

What if I grow a beard overnight?
What if a vampire gives me a bite?

What if I'm woken by a scream?
What if it's *real* and not a dream?

At night-time, as I lie in bed,
The Worries swirl around my head.

John Foster

■ SCHOLASTIC

UNIT 4

Non-fiction

Interpreting instructions is one of the main reading skills needed to function successfully in life. When children are taught to organise instructions in different ways depending upon audience and purpose, they are also learning how to be analytical readers of instructions.

The process of taking notes and interpreting these at a later date is also an important life skill that needs to be learned. Laying foundations in primary school for a skill that will be used so extensively in later education is particularly important given that note-taking habits of adults can prove extremely difficult to break. An excess of writing frames can set up a dependency culture and instead visual learners are encouraged here to use pictures and create their own tables for information gathering and note taking. This method of note-taking also helps to focus the reader, listener or observer when specific information is required.

In preparation for the unit, collect examples of instructions from everyday life, such as recipes, game rules, instructions for electronic equipment and so on, and ask the children to do the same.

Hours 2 and 3 tie in with Unit 13 of *Grammar for Writing*.

Hour	Shared text-level work	Shared word-/ sentence-level work	Guided and independent work	Plenary
1 A flying start	Reading a variety of instructional texts, identifying purposes.		Following different instructions for the same product.	Discussing which instructions were most successful and how others could have been improved.
2 Dinosaurs (1)	Discussing the purpose of note taking; reducing a sentence to the main meaning.	Identifying non-essential words, noting adverbs.	Deleting unnecessary information from sentences in note-taking.	Using notes to answer questions in a quiz.
3 Dinosaurs (2)	Trying two examples of extracting key information.	Experimenting with which words can be deleted.	Making notes from two paragraphs of text to condense the whole text into one paragraph.	Evaluating condensed texts; checking they are in children's own words.
4 Dinosaurs (3)	Taking notes as you impart information orally.	Writing quickly and fluently.	Making a table to take notes; using the table to answer questions.	Quiz to test notes on tables; discussing difficulties.
5 Monster sandwich	Taking notes as you make a sandwich; organising written instructions.		Using notes to write instructions as a list of numbered steps.	Having another class test instructions; modifying accordingly.

UNIT 4

Hour	Shared text-level work	Shared word-/ sentence-level work	Guided reading/ writing	Independent work	Plenary
6 A perfect birthday	Looking at flow charts; working to reorder muddled instructions as a flow chart.		Reorganising muddled instructions into a flow chart.	Checking order of instructions; revising sequence words.	Matching word cards to words on the board; identifying sounds with various spellings.
7 Capturing castles	Modelling how to take notes on main points from a passage of information, transferring these to a table.		Taking notes from a passage; re-organising these as instructions (children choose method of organising instructions).	Sharing instructions.	Sharing couplets; focusing on long-vowel digraphs and rhymes.
8 Designing a board game	Considering the criteria for making a board game.	Revising second-person and present-tense nature of instructions.	Deciding theme and bonuses/forfeits for game.	Sharing ideas and providing peer support.	Reading and discussing new verses, focusing on rhyme.
9 Making the game	Setting instructions/ tasks for making the game.	Noting the importance of clear handwriting; revising dictionary skills.	Making the game; playing a test game.	Quality Assurance teams comment on the games.	Discussing different uses of capital letters.
10 Quality assurance	Discussing various ways to write game rules.		Playing the game; drafting rules/ instructions; swapping games for troubleshooting the rules.	Making changes in the light of advice.	Sharing poems, focusing on spelling and discussing how punctuation affects reading.

Key assessment opportunities
● Can the children follow instructions presented in a variety of ways?
● Can they extract the main point from a sentence?
● Can they write a set of instructions that can be followed by another child?
● Can they use sequencing words and imperative verbs?

A flying start

Objectives

NLS
T12: To identify the different purposes of instructional text.
T13: To discuss the merits and limitations of particular instructional texts and to compare these with others.
T14: To learn how written instructions are organised.
T15: To read and follow instructions.

What you need
- Examples of instructions brought in by the children (and/or you)
- photocopiable page 127
- 1cm squared paper
- scissors
- paper clips.

Shared text-level work
- Display the instructions you and the children have brought. Discuss the purposes of the different kinds of instructions, for example, on a food packet telling how to cook the meal, how to assemble a piece of furniture, or safety instructions for using candles, how to play computer and board games, using a help facility in ICT, pictorial references in PE.
- Point out how different instructions are organised using pictures, numbered lists, bullet points and flow charts and discuss how each is useful in its own way. For example, diagrams are more appropriate than lots of text for furniture assembly.

Guided and independent work
- Divide the class into three groups to make paper helicopters. Give Group 1 the diagrams, Group 2 the text and Group 3 both sets of instructions. Tell the groups to work together to follow their instructions and not to talk to other groups. Allow about twenty minutes for constructing the paper helicopters.
- Now help the children to test their helicopters. If there is a high point in the school, such as an upstairs balcony or small window from which the helicopters can be safely dropped and observed, this is ideal. If not, help children to stand on a chair and drop their helicopters from an upstretched hand.

Plenary
- Ask each group in turn how difficult they found the task and how well their helicopters worked. Were their instructions useful and easy to follow? Group 3 will have found the task easiest because they had a combination of diagrams and text. Did Group 1 encounter any significant problems? How 'wordy' did Group 2 find the text? Did they find it difficult to keep track of where they were in step 1? Did any of the helicopters fail because of difficulty with the instructions?
- Elicit that a briefly captioned/annotated diagram of each instruction would have been the most helpful presentation method.
- Tell the children to look out for examples of instructions presented in this way and encourage them to add examples to the display at any time during the week.
- Over the week, encourage the children to reorganise the instructions on the wall into sets with common features. Allow this to be an ongoing activity for early finishers. Not all of the publications will fit neatly into categories as they will contain a range of instruction presentations.
- Make this an interactive feature of the display by encouraging the children to find new ways of categorising and reorganising the sets of the instructions.

Differentiation

Less able
- Provide children with a template ready to be cut out and assembled.

More able
- Early finishers can decorate their completed helicopters before testing.

Dinosaurs (1)

Objectives

NLS
T17: To make clear notes.
S9: to experiment with deleting words in sentences to see which are essential to retain meaning and which are not.
W13: To recognise and spell common suffixes and how these influence word meanings.

S&L
31 Group discussion and interaction: To actively include and respond to all members of the group.

Shared work

● Brainstorm situations in which it might be useful to make notes, for example, in a group discussion, when listening to someone give information, when extracting information from a text.

● Tell the children that notes should contain only the important information and do not need to be written in sentences. Unimportant words can be left out. Write the following sentence on the board:

> Some dinosaurs with terrifying jaws greedily ate raw flesh while other dinosaurs lived happily on green plants and leaves.

● Consider which words are necessary to retain meaning. Offer the eraser to children to rub out one or two words at a time. Elicit that adjectives and adverbs can nearly always be removed when making notes (although it may depend on what the notes are being made for). Remind the children that any word ending in the suffix *ly* is an adverb.

● With the sentence reduced, ask the children how to reduce it even further to put it into note form, for example, *Dinosaurs – flesh/plants*.

Guided and independent work

● Write the following sentences on the board and tell the children to put each sentence into note form:

> ● Many people are interested in dinosaurs because they were such amazing animals, but a person who actually tries to find out about different life forms from long ago by studying ancient fossils is called a palaeontologist.
> ● Dinosaur fossils have been found throughout history, but before the 1840s people did not really know what they were and so discoveries of dinosaur bones often gave rise to stories about dragons and monsters.
> ● Although we often see grey, brown or green dinosaurs in books and on television, we have no real photographs of them, and no dinosaur skin has survived, so dinosaurs could have been pink or yellow or bright blue with red dots for all we know.

● Encourage discussion between pairs as they consider what information to retain. The critical thinking involved in discussion is extremely valuable, even if final decisions are mistaken.

● Now combine the pairs into groups of four. Ask these new groups to compare notes and decide on the best notes for each sentence.

Differentiation

Less able
● Assist children in reducing the three sentences to note form using the same strategy demonstrated.

More able
● Select a more complex text for children to take notes from.

Plenary

● Ask the children the following questions:

> 1. What do we call a scientist who studies dinosaurs?
> 2. What did people often think long ago when they found dinosaur bones?
> 3. What colour were dinosaurs?

● Ask each group to read out their corresponding notes after each question. Congratulate those groups with good answers.

Dinosaurs (2)

Objectives

NLS
T17: To make clear notes.
S9: To experiment with deleting words from sentences to see which are essential to retain meaning and which are not.

What you need
● Photocopiable page 128.

Shared text- and sentence-level work
● Tell the children that different kinds of note-taking are useful in different situations. Ask what methods they might use if given a piece of text to extract key information from. Suggest, for example, underlining, highlighting and circling of words, perhaps annotating in the margins, as well as writing down short phrases and noting ideas into their own words.
● Read the first two paragraphs of photocopiable page 128 with the children. Tell them that there are two main points being made and see if they can establish what they are:

> 1. The last dinosaurs died out 65 million years ago, some having been around for 180 million years.
> 2. They lived all over the world.

● Point out to the children that often in information passages, although not always, each paragraph will contain one main point. Ask the children which essential words they would write down to represent each point.
● Elicit dinosaurs were around for *180 million* years, and the last dinosaurs died *65 million* years ago *(180 + 65 = 245)* from paragraph 1 and *lived everywhere* from paragraph 2.
● Emphasise to the children the importance of using their own words when writing up their notes. The concept of plagiarism could be explained at this stage if appropriate.
● Ask the children to help you to develop your notes into new sentences, for example:

> 1. Dinosaurs lived from 245 million years ago to 65 million years ago.
> 2. Dinosaurs lived on every part of the earth.

● Ask the children to copy these sentences to begin a paragraph of their own report about dinosaurs.
● Read the rest of the text to the children.

Guided and independent work
● Organise mixed-ability pairs, giving each pair photocopiable page 128. Remind them that there is one main point in each paragraph. Tell the children to underline those points in paragraphs 3 and 4 and to make notes by writing a few words to represent each one.
● Now ask the children, working individually, to write a sentence for each set of words they have noted. When these are added to the first two sentences, the children will find that they have written a short paragraph about dinosaurs.

Differentiation

Less able
● Provide sentences with appropriate gaps to be filled.

More able
● Ask children to write sentences from notes taken from the more complex text in Hour 3.

Plenary
● Ask volunteers to read out their paragraphs. Invite comments from the rest of the class. Have the children captured the main points about dinosaurs from the original text? Are the paragraphs written in their own words?

Dinosaurs (3)

Objectives

NLS
T17: To make clear notes.
W27: To build up handwriting speed, fluency and legibility through practice.

What you need
● Photocopiable page 129.

Shared text- and word-level work
● Tell the children that today they will learn and practise how to take notes when listening for particular pieces of information. Say that you will read them a short passage about a dinosaur and that they should know the name, size, appearance and diet of the dinosaur when you have finished. Give out scrap paper for them to jot notes down as you read. When the children are ready, read aloud the text at the top of photocopiable page 129.
● Ask the children the name of the dinosaur, how big it was, what it looked like and what it ate. Ask them how easy they found it to hear and note the facts and then make use of the facts. Consider how much more difficult the task would be if there were four different dinosaurs and they had to be able to state the name, size, appearance and diet of each by the end of the passage.

Guided and independent work
● Explain that one way to make the task easier is to use a table. Draw the table below on the board for the children to copy. Tell them to draw the table freehand, (as they will often be taking notes when they do not have a ruler to hand or have time to use one), leaving plenty of space in each box for their notes.

Dinosaur	Size	Appearance	Diet
Stegosaurus	bus	Bone plates on back, spikes on tail	plants

● Explain to the children that you will now read out a second, longer passage, and you want them to fill in the table with the appropriate information. Warn the children that they will need to be alert, focused and swift in noting main points of information into the appropriate sections of the table.
● Stress that careful handwriting is not important in this task. They will need to be able to read the notes, so handwriting must be legible, but it is speed, not beauty that matters in note-taking!
● Read the rest of photocopiable page 129.

Differentiation

Less able
● Read the longer text two or three times and provide these children with a table already drawn for them.

More able
● Children should research and add to the table. Challenge them to find information on two more dinosaurs.

Plenary
● Ask the children ten questions which will elicit the information from the completed chart. For example, *How big was Apatosaurus? Which dinosaurs ate meat?*
● Complete the table on the board by using the children's answers.
● Children scoring ten points have obviously taken very good notes. Discuss what was difficult and easy in carrying out the task.

Monster sandwich

Shared text-level work

● Remind the children of the instructions displayed at the beginning of the unit. Draw attention to any recipes. Tell the children that they will be writing instructions on how to make a monster sandwich. While you demonstrate the process first, they should make notes of the things you say and do that will be useful when writing the instructions.

● Place the ingredients on a table, and talk the children through the process of making the sandwich. (Make sure that step 1 is to wash your hands.) Use a variety of ingredients, both to make the instruction-writing more challenging, and to keep the children amused and interested! Cocktail sticks might be used to hold the finished product together. An extra slice of bread in the middle of the sandwich can give it increased stability!

● Leaving the sandwich and ingredients on display for the children to see, tell them that you want them to write instructions on how it was made so that another person could make an identical sandwich. Assure them that the sandwich is absolutely delicious and that such a set of instructions may well prove very useful!

● Ask how the instructions should begin. (A list of ingredients or *What you need*.) Elicit each step orally to ensure the children have a clear idea of the steps and the order in which they were carried out. Briefly discuss what would happen if they got the order of steps wrong!

● Consider how the instructions might be set out on paper. Direct the children to the use of a numbered sequence of steps. Write:

> 1. Wash your hands.
> 2. Butter three slices of bread.

● Point out that the instructions you have supplied start with a verb 'ordering' the reader to do something. Tell them that they should continue this pattern in their instructions.

Guided and independent work

● Ask the children to use their notes to write the instructions in simple numbered steps. Tell them that the best workers will be rewarded with a bite of the monster sandwich! Before any of the children handle or eat any of the food, check that none of them have any special dietary requirements or related food allergies.

Plenary

● The best way to test any set of instructions, and to demonstrate that instructions do have an important purpose, is to follow them. Give the finished instructions, along with the necessary ingredients, to another class and ask those children to make monster sandwiches. The authors of the instructions should watch in silence as the other children attempt to replicate the original sandwich.

● After this frustrating experience, discuss with the children what went wrong and how they might have improved their instructions!

A perfect birthday

Objectives

NLS
T14: To learn how written instructions are organised.
T15: To read and follow simple instructions.

What you need
● Photocopiable pages 130 and 131.

Shared text-level work
● Tell the children that another way of presenting instructions is in the form of a flow chart – a series of boxes, each containing an instruction, linked to the next box with an arrow. Show any examples that you have already on display.
● Explain that the editor of *Child* magazine, which gives news and advice to parents, has dropped the instructions for giving a child the perfect birthday and these are now mixed up in the wrong order. Tell the children that the editor wants their help to organise a flow chart of the instructions in the correct order.
● Read through the muddled instructions on photocopiable page 130 with the children.
● Draw a box at the top of the board, large enough to contain one of the instructions and ask the children which instruction comes first. How can they tell? Write it in, then draw an arrow from the first box to a second box and ask the children which instruction comes next. Continue through the instructions, but abbreviate the instructions into short phrases, taking advice from the children (for example, *Get up at dawn*).
● Tell the children to put the appropriate number next to each instruction as it is written into the flow chart. In this way it is easy to see which ones have not been used yet.
● One instruction is incomplete. Discuss what options the children would choose for this instruction. Once agreed, add it to the chart.

Guided and independent work
● Organise the children into pairs and distribute photocopiable page 131, so that they can arrange to give you a perfect day! Read through the sheet with the children.
● Now tell them to cut out the instructions and arrange them in the correct order.
● When they are satisfied with the order, tell the pairs to stick the instructions onto a sheet of paper and to add arrows to show the correct sequence.

Plenary
● Check the sequence of instructions and ask the children to explain how they knew the correct order. Elicit that there are sequencing words that indicate the order in which instructions happen: *first, second, next, then, finally, after that*. The order of other instructions on the sheet has been indicated through content.
● It may be worthwhile practice to let the children cut out and order photocopiable page 130. The results could be taken home and shared with parents!
● An alternative is for the children to design their own personal birthday flow chart to take home.

Differentiation

Less able
● Number the instructions with the children before they cut and stick.

More able
● A group could make a flow chart for giving pupils a perfect day at school.

Capturing castles

Shared text-level work

● Distribute photocopiable page 132, read it to the children and check their understanding. Tell them that their task will be to extract the methods by which castles were conquered during the Middle Ages.
● Ask the children which paragraphs contain the information they are looking for. (Paragraphs 2, 3, 4 and 5.) Encourage the children to explain how they found the information. Did they scan for key words?
● Tell the children to circle key words and phrases in the third paragraph which explains how King Robert the Bruce captured Perth castle. Draw a simple table like this on the board:

Castle	How it was captured
Perth	

● Ask the children to volunteer the words and phrases they have underlined. Add to the table those which describe how the castle was taken, for example, *moat only up to man's neck; climbed walls.* Demonstrate how key words form a set of notes.

Guided and independent work

● Ask the children to copy the table from the board and to repeat the note-making process for the other three castles - highlighting the relevant words and writing them into their own tables. There is no information on how King Robert captured Stirling castle, and the children should therefore leave this box blank.
● Then collect in their copies of the text. Tell the children that they are going to write the instructions the young Bruce might have given to his men before they attacked Edinburgh castle. Discuss the following organisational methods with the children and then tell them that they have five minutes to make their decisions individually:

● Bullet points, numbered instructions, flow-charts or annotated drawings?
● Each sentence/phrase to begin with a verb in the second person or a sequencing word such as *first, next, after that, lastly?*

● Ask the children to begin their instructions with this introduction:

We are in luck. We know of a secret pathway at the back of the castle. These are the instructions for how we'll capture this castle:

● In groups, ask the children to imagine they are knights in the Middle Ages and plan to capture a castle. They should decide how they will organise their instructions and write these for sharing with the class.

Plenary

● Share and compare ideas for capturing a castle. Which do the children think would be successful?

📖 **123**

Designing a board game

Shared text-level work
● Tell the children that they are going to make a board game to be played by children of the same age or one year younger. Write the following details on the board and go through them with the children:

> ● The game will be played on a board with 100 squares.
> ● It will be played with a dice.
> ● There will be counters for four players.
> ● Certain squares on the board will be marked with a simple picture which corresponds with a picture on the back of one of the cards.
> ● The card will give an instruction for moving forward or back a certain number of squares.
> ● There will be 20 picture squares and 20 cards with matching pictures on the back.

● Ask the children to suggest themes/settings for their games, such as the playground, a theme park, a castle capture. Choose a school trip for the shared game. Squares need to be drawn and numbered and a start and finish square marked. The game cards will have to be made. For the school trip game, they might be marked as follows:

> ● Coach breaks down. Go back 10 squares (picture of flat tyre on card and square).
> ● You arrive at the zoo. Move forward 8 squares (picture of sign 'Welcome to the zoo').
> ● The zoo is not open for another hour. Go back 2 squares (picture of closed gates).

● Ask the children to decide ten positive ideas to send players forward and ten negative things to send players back.
● Elicit ideas for cards in a football theme, for example, players run onto the field, team scores a goal, a player is injured, a penalty has been given to the opposition.

Shared sentence-level work
● Note that game instructions are written in the second person (directly address) and in the present tense. Ask the children to pick out the imperative verbs mentioned: *Go, Move* and so on.

Guided and independent work
● Organise the children into groups of five and allow five minutes to decide the theme for their game. Allow a further fifteen minutes to brainstorm ten bonus and ten forfeit cards. Explain that they will make the game in the next lesson.
● Circulate to hear some of the discussions.

Plenary
● Ask each group to give a progress report. Encourage discussion of themes that are not working and how to change them.

Making the game

Objectives

NLS
T15: To read and follow simple instructions.
T16: To write instructions, eg rules for playing games.
W5: To identify mis-spelt words in own writing.
W22: To know the quartiles of the dictionary.

S&L
27 Group discussion and interaction: To use talk to organise roles and action.

What you need
- Squared paper
- small cards
- correction fluid or sticky labels
- dice and counters.

Shared text-level work
- Remind the children of the themes and game cards they thought of in Hour 8. Today the board game must be completed and group members will have to work together, agreeing and carrying out the many tasks that remain to be done.
- Identify the order in which tasks should be performed, listing them on the board.

> 1. Re-read the game cards and improve them if necessary.
> 2. Check there are ten bonuses and ten forfeits.
> 3. Establish the number of squares to move forward and backward for each card.
> 4. Decide which squares on the board will correspond to a game card.
> 5. Each child will take responsibility for making four cards and deciding pictures.
> 6. The first child to finish writing cards should number the squares on the board.
> 7. Pictures must be drawn on the cards and the corresponding squares on the board.
> 8. *Start* and *Finish* squares should be marked.
> 9. Decide how to start playing the game, for example, throwing a 6 or highest score goes first.

Shared word-level work
- Tell the children that it is important that their handwriting is neat and they have checked their spellings are correct so that other people are to be able to play the game.
- Suggest that before writing onto the game cards, group members check their draft spellings. Encourage them to check with each other and a dictionary.
- Revise dictionary quartile skills: to find words quickly remember that words beginning with *m* lie in the middle and *t* comes towards the end and so on.

Guided and independent work
- Tell the children that this is a challenge to see which groups can follow verbal and written instructions. Those groups that design and complete a playable game in line with the criteria will have passed the test. Organise a chairperson for each group and remind him or her to keep people on task. A timekeeper should give regular time checks up to the limit of thirty minutes.
- When the tasks have been completed, ask the groups to play the game as a test run. This is the fine tuning part of the process! If game board squares need to be changed, this could be done either with correction fluid or by sticking a small label over the mistake.

Differentiation

Less able
- Children should be allocated the task of timekeeper and told to inform the group after every five minutes. Prompt them if necessary.

More able
- Good organisers and able collaborative workers should have the complex job of chairperson.

Plenary
- Arrange the games in a circle around the classroom and allow groups to look for a few minutes at other people's games. Positive comments should be invited as the first part of the Quality Assurance process.

Quality assurance

Objectives

NLS
T13: To discuss the merits and limitations of particular instructional texts.
T16: To write instructions, eg rules for playing games.
W19: To use dictionaries to check the spellings of words.
W27: To build up handwriting speed, fluency and legibility.

What you need
● The children's board games
● dice and counters.

Shared text-level work
● Tell the children that today they will be writing the full instructions/game rules for their games. Ask: *What is the first thing players need to know?* (What is needed: dice, counters and so on.) After this, the groups will have to explain in writing exactly how to play the game. Tell them to imagine that they are players who have never seen the game before.
● Remind the children how instructions may be written, for example:

● numbered or bulleted list
● flow chart
● annotated diagrams.

● Ask the groups to decide which is most appropriate for their game.

Guided and independent work
● Explain that the best way to identify the instructions needed is to play the game in slow motion, with every group member noting what is done at each stage. Building up speed, fluency and legibility is a handwriting skill that is essential and this type of task is a perfect opportunity for all children to gain practice. The children have been taught how to make brief notes, rather than always writing whole sentences and this is an appropriate occasion for this skill to be used.
● After playing a couple of rounds of the game, tell individuals to make their own list of instructions in rough draft form. While waiting for all group members to complete the task, tell the children to check their own spellings, underlining words about which they have doubts and then checking these in the dictionary. Stress that if new players come to the game and cannot read the words because of incorrect spelling, then the instructions will be of no use.
● When all group members have a complete set of game rules, ask the groups to pool the instructions and discuss and choose the best. Allow a little time to make improvements if there are points from other sets that would make the chosen one even better.
● Swap the games amongst the groups and tell the children that they are now Quality Assurance teams checking the game rules. As the children attempt to play the games, one group member should note recommended changes where necessary.
● Return the games and annotated instructions.

Differentiation

Less able
● Support children in organising the individual rules for their games.
● Check spelling and punctuation.

More able
● Good writers should be identified as group scribes.
● Children with good ICT skills should word-process the instructions.

Plenary
● Ask the groups to comment upon one another's instructions and games and to decide if the group whose game they played has passed the quality assurance test!
● Let the children make any necessary final changes and to word-process the game rules. Game boards, cards and instructions could then be laminated.
● If possible, groups could play their games with younger classes.

Paper helicopter

Group 1

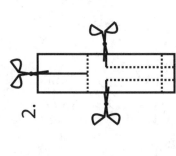

1.

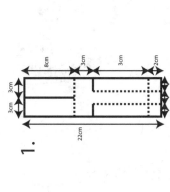

2.

3.

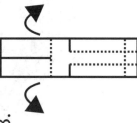

4.

5.

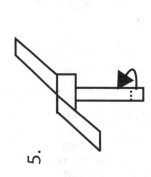

6.

Group 2

1. Draw a rectangle 6cm wide and 22cm high. Draw an 8cm vertical line from the centre of the top line of the rectangle towards the centre. Label this line A. Draw a horizontal line across the rectangle to touch the end of line A. Label this line B. Draw another horizontal line 2cm below line B. Label this line C. Measure 2cm along C from the left and make a mark. Draw a line down from this mark to the bottom of the rectangle. Label this line D. Measure 2cm along C from the right and make a mark. Draw a line from this to the bottom of the rectangle. Label this line E. Erase the part of line C that runs between D and E. Draw a line across the rectangle 2cm up from the bottom. Label this line F.

2. Cut along line A and the two remaining parts of line C.

3. Fold the flaps along line B in opposite directions.

4. Fold along D and E to produce a long thin tail.

5. Fold up the bottom of the tail along line F.

6. Attach a paperclip to the end of the tail to hold things in place and add weight.

Now hold your helicopter high and let it go. It will spin as it falls.

Dinosaurs – when and where

Everyone knows that there are no dinosaurs still alive today, but few people realise just how long ago they roamed the earth and how long they were the main animals on the planet. The last dinosaurs died out 65 million years ago, with some species having been around for 180 million years. These big numbers are hard to comprehend, but when you realise that the first humans, more like apes than the people of today, appeared about 2 million years ago, you get an idea of just how much time is involved.

As for *where* the dinosaurs lived, the answer is that they lived all over the world. Many dinosaurs could swim, and still more lived in the water. When the dinosaurs lived, there were no continents – all the land on the Earth was stuck together. Dinosaurs, therefore, did not have water to cross like we have today. They could walk anywhere.

No one knows for certain why the dinosaurs died out. We know that there were lots of volcanoes and earthquakes, but they would not be enough to kill off all the dinosaurs. Most scientists believe that a huge asteroid hit the Earth. This caused a dust cloud that covered the sun for years. This change in climate meant the dinosaurs could no longer survive.

However, maybe not all dinosaurs died out. Animals evolve over millions of years. Some dinosaurs were very like birds, and many scientists think that they may have evolved into the birds that fly around in our skies today.

Dinosaurs – sizes and shapes

Stegosaurus was about the size of a single-deck bus. It had two rows of bony plates running down its back and for extra protection it had four large spikes at the end of its long tail. Although it must have looked fearsome, Stegosaurus was not as dangerous as many other dinosaurs as it ate only plants, which it swallowed without chewing.

Triceratops, a plant-eating dinosaur, grew to about ten metres long and three metres tall. It had a bony plate on the back of its skull and three horns coming from its face. Triceratops probably lived in herds. It needed all the protection it

could get because it was hunted by the Tyrannosaurus Rex, possibly the fiercest dinosaur of all. Tyrannosaurus was about twelve metres long and six metres tall. It stood on two legs, and its long tail helped it to balance. It had a huge head with powerful jaws and around fifty sharp teeth. These dinosaurs were big, but some where much bigger. The giant Apatosaurus, also called Brontosaurus, was about twenty seven metres long and four to five metres tall. It was one of the most unintelligent dinosaurs, with a tiny brain. It ate leaves and plants, and also ate stones to help with its digestion. It walked on four legs and had a very long tail and a very long neck. Other dinosaurs were quite small. Compsognathus, a small and very fast meat-eater that looked like a miniature Tyrannosaurus, was about the size of a chicken.

How to give your child the perfect birthday

Be sure to be out of bed as the dawn breaks. (Your child will be up very early.)

Serve your child with the three-course lunch of crisps, chocolate cake and ice cream.

Before arranging the presents, ask your child to jump on the bed for ten minutes.

Arrange the pile of presents very carefully. (You don't want your child to be crushed if they fall.)

After clearing up the wrapping paper, remember to laugh kindly when your child refuses to eat porridge for breakfast.

Arrange to be out by 7.00pm when your child's 20 guests arrive.

In between breakfast and lunch ring McFly to check that they are playing at tonight's party.

Secondly, get washed and, put the soap away. (Your child will not be using it today.)

Finally, don't forget to leave your car keys with the chauffeur hired for the day.

After lunch and before the shopping visit the zoo.

Give your child your credit card for a visit to the trainer shop.

Whilst in the shopping centre, remember to order two unsuitable horror DVDs.

How to give your teacher a perfect day

Take the healthy option for lunch, choosing the salad, rather than the chips.

Enter the classroom in silence.

After lunch, adjust the pillow under the teacher's head.

After playtime, bow politely to the teacher and get out your reading.

Volunteer to tidy the cupboards during break.

Before going home be sure to polish the teacher's shoes.

Before lunch, ask the teacher if you can have a spelling test instead of art.

Thirdly, be sure to completely ignore your friend when s/he tries to tell you a secret.

While the teacher is having a nap, work in silence.

Offer the teacher your snack. You know she likes a nice bar of chocolate.

Sit down, rub the sleep out of your eyes and complete the maths test.

TERM 2

Capturing castles

Between 1307 and 1314 King Robert the Bruce and his men recaptured about 130 Scottish castles. Some castles were surrounded and the occupants starved out. Others were taken by assault. Eventually, only the four biggest castles remained. They were Berwick, Perth, Edinburgh, and Stirling. Bruce had no big siege-engines or battering-rams, and so he had to be clever, using the element of surprise.

Bruce sent his brother to take Berwick castle, and they had a clever plan. It was attacked at night. A rope ladder was made with a grappling hook at the end. The soldiers threw it over the high wall and climbed up the rope. Once the men were inside they surprised the sleeping soldiers and took over the castle.

Perth castle had a moat around it. A moat was often as wide and as deep as a river. The soldiers inside the castle felt safe, but Bruce asked one of his men to find out how deep the water was. It only came up to the man's neck. The next night Bruce led a few of his men right through the water and they managed to climb over the castle walls and let down the drawbridge. Bruce's men flooded in and soon took over the castle.

Robert the Bruce's nephew was given the job of taking Edinburgh castle. Luckily, one of his men had been a soldier there many years before. He had discovered a secret pathway down the cliffs at the back of the castle which he had used to visit his girlfriend in the town at night. Bruce's nephew sent most of his men to the front of the castle as a diversion. The soldiers were fooled and only defended the front wall. Meanwhile, a few of Bruce's nephew's best fighters climbed the cliffs and hacked their way through a small wooden door at the back of the castle. Once inside, they were able to raise the portcullis and let in the rest of the Scots.

Finally, only one big castle remained to be taken: Stirling...

ALL NEW 100 LITERACY HOURS · YEAR 3

◼ SCHOLASTIC

UNIT 1

Narrative: perspective/ character

This study of dialogue, character and perspective uses a narrative poem by Allan Ahlberg, 'Talk Us Through It Charlotte', in which a girl explains how she scored the winning goal for her brother's football team. The children explore the idea of perspective by exploring the feelings of other players and writing a commentary on the game. Then, they write their own personal narrative accounts of their first day of school and consider how these reflect their personalities and the different ways they see the world. These should be written in a format suitable for parents to read and discuss with their children. The children also explore writing dialogue and build a base for future work by constructing a thematic dictionary of synonyms for *said*. Hour 4 covers Unit 15 in *Grammar for Writing*.

Hour	Shared text-level work	Shared word-/sentence-level work	Guided and independent work	Plenary
1 Charlotte's goal	Reading a poem and visualising events and characters.		Making a character feelings map; writing a character profile.	Discussing differences in the character maps; re-reading the poem.
2 The commentator	Re-reading the poem; distinguishing between first and third person accounts.	Identifying personal pronouns.	Writing a football commentary using key events identified.	Performing some of the commentaries; discussing the player and commentator viewpoints.
3 Character dialogues		Revising how to write and punctuate dialogue; discussing impact of some synonyms for *said*.	Playing a game to generate dialogue ideas, using different synonyms for *said*.	Sharing conversations; collecting more *said* synonyms; publishing work.
4 Synonyms for *said*		Editing a dialogue for pronouns and synonyms of *said*.	Collecting synonyms in a booklet; editing conversations from Hour 3.	Comparing editing decisions and classifications.
5 First day at school	Describing personalities; discussing how personality affects what we do and how we see events.		Recalling and writing about first day at school; talking about personalities.	Sharing accounts and discussing how people react differently to situations

Key assessment opportunities
● Can the children visualise as they read?
● Do they find it easy to speculate and to empathise with characters' feelings?
● Do they read with expression?
● Can they maintain the third-person in narrative writing?
● Do they punctuate speech and dialogue correctly?

Charlotte's goal

Objectives

NLS
T3: To distinguish between 1st and 3rd person accounts.
T5: To discuss character's feelings; behaviour; relationships, referring to the text and making judgements.

What you need

● Photocopiable page 139.

Shared text-level work

● Introduce the poem on photocopiable page 139 by reminding the children that football players are often interviewed after a match and asked to describe the goals. In this poem Charlotte is doing just this.
● Read the poem. Explain that good readers speculate about characters, and everyone will imagine Charlotte differently. Ask the children: What sort of a girl do they think Charlotte is? What clothes might she wear? What might her brother have said to her before and after the match? Explain that readers could draw parallels between Charlotte and people they know in real life or other story characters.

Guided and independent work

● Ask the children to read the poem aloud in pairs, encouraging them to adopt Charlotte's voice. Ask them to visualise each event as it occurs.
● Explain that they are going to make a 'character feelings map' to show what some characters think and feel about one another. They should write the main characters (Charlotte, her brother, her friend) spaced-out across A3 paper and write brief notes about how each character felt before, during and after the match. Evidence for this may come from the poem or be inferred. Encourage speculation about what each character hopes for and what they are thinking about.
● Then ask the children to speculate about how the characters view each other. Tell them to draw an arrowed line to connect one character to another. Along the line they should write this character's relationship to the other person, any key things they say or do with them and what they probably think about them. This should result in 9 lines.

Charlotte	Before:	I might as well have a go.
	During:	I'm bored. I'm keeping the ball.
	After:	I enjoyed that! That showed them.
Friend	Before:	Is he looking at me? Does my hair look good?
	During:	I'm cold. There's no one to talk to.
	After:	Charlotte did well. He *is* looking at me.
Brother	Before:	Hope we win. Charlotte's going to muck it up and the boys will blame me.
	During:	Why won't she pass?
	After:	I'm not sure I want Charlotte to be in the team.

● Ask each child to write a short prose description of one of the characters. Tell them to write in the third person – writing as someone watching the character not as the character him/herself.

Plenary

● Display and compare the maps produced. Use the descriptions to generate further discussion about what we can know for certain from the text and what we imagine.
● Re-read the poem. Do the children imagine characters differently?

Differentiation

Less able
● Ask children to describe the poem's events in their own words, making it as realistic as they can. Use a writing frame to ensure they do not lapse into the first person.

More able
● Encourage children to include memorable images in their description of events.

The commentator

Objectives

NLS
T3: Distinguish between 1st and 3rd person accounts.
S2: To identify pronouns and understand their functions in sentences.

S&L
36 Drama: To use some drama strategies to explore stories.

What you need
● Photocopiable page 139.

Differentiation

Less able
● For less able children, or those less familiar with sport commentaries, construct a class list of phrases for reference during their talk.
● Encourage them to have a go at writing, but if some find it impossible to get started, provide a lead-in: *And the ball's gone to their new player. She's...*

More able
● Expect more able children to write a lengthier piece, with some descriptive phrases about how Charlotte moves.

Shared text- and sentence-level work
● Remind the children of the poem and re-read it together.
● Explain that one reason the poem is so interesting and immediate is because it is a first person account – Charlotte gives us her view of the game. We get an insight into her personality and thoughts.
● Demonstrate the use of the first person by going through the initial verses of the poem in detail, annotating the text to identify all the personal views and comments Charlotte makes, and the uses of *I, me* or *my*. Note also the 'childish', colloquial, informal, chatty language appropriate to a young girl speaking. How accurate do they think Charlotte's report of the game is?
● Discuss how the same match would be reported differently by a football commentator, who would give a more even-handed commentary focused on Charlotte's actions and the skills involved. What language would be used then? (It would be more formal, with pronouns *he, she, they, them* and so on.)

Guided and independent work
● Tell the children to provide a football commentary on the match. Explain that they will need to describe what happens and add their own views and comments about the way that the game is going.
● To start them off, organise the children into pairs and ask them to discuss what actually happened in this part of the match. Ask them to read each verse and write a short note to indicate the events that a football commentator describing the match might report.
Remind them to change the pronouns.
● Give the pairs a chance to rehearse their writing by developing an oral commentary on the match.
● Then, ask the children to write a commentary individually. Suggest that their first sentence(s) should set the scene by describing the positions of the players in relation to the ball, at the point Charlotte becomes involved.

Plenary
● Ask some of the children to perform their commentaries, with appropriate style and tone if possible.
● Discuss the differences between the commentator's perspective and Charlotte's – someone directly involved in the action and someone watching from 'outside' (first and third person).
● Encourage the children to think about other stories they have read that are told from the character's perspective (stories by Jacqueline Wilson and Dick King-Smith, for example, often do this) and from a third person narrator's perspective (most fairy tales, fables and Rudyard Kipling's *Just So Stories*, for instance). Discuss why authors might choose one or the other and how each can be a powerful form.
● Ask the children to note the perspective in the next story they read or hear.

Character dialogues

Objectives

NLS
S4: To use speech marks and other dialogue punctuation appropriately and the conventions which mark boundaries between spoken words and the rest of the sentence.
W13: To collect synonyms which will be useful in writing dialogue.

What you need
● Photocopiable page 140.

Shared text-level work
● Recap that speech marks help readers to know when someone is speaking. Say that an easy way to remember how to write speech marks: imagine that what the character says is in a speech bubble, but only write the top left and top right bits of the bubble – at the beginning and end of what the character says.
● Explain that dialogue is important because it can tell us about the personality of the characters that are speaking. Readers sometimes need help to know how people are speaking. Writers often give clues about the characters' feelings by using synonyms for *said*.
● Quickly brainstorm some synonyms for *said* and write these on the board for reference throughout the lesson.

Guided and independent work
● Explain that the group are going to play a dialogue game in pairs. Cut up the character names from the top half of the photocopiable sheet and put them into a box.
● Give each pair a context from the sheet. Explain that this is the situation in which the characters meet. Then ask each child to pick a name from the character box.
● Tell the children to work with their partner to devise a dialogue between their two characters. Why are they there? How do they feel about the situation? How do they feel about each other? What might they say? How would they speak? Once children have talked in general terms, ask them to invent the conversation that takes place.
● Ask the children to work individually to write the conversation between their characters.
● Remind them of the conventions for writing dialogue and of why/ when they might want to use synonyms for *said*. To set the scene for the conversations, children could be given the following sentence starter: *One day*, (character 1) *met* (character 2) *when they were* (context) *and this is how the conversation went…*
● Once finished, let the children read and edit their own work.

Plenary
● Share the conversations that children have written, encouraging authors to read in appropriate voices and accents.
● After a conversation has been read aloud, ask the other children to identify effective use of dialogue to convey the characters' feelings and personalities, and effective use of synonyms for *said*.
● Explain that there are many synonyms for *said*, far more than the class has collected. Ask the children to write a list for homework by brainstorming their own ideas, looking at books and asking their family.
● Once edited to ensure that the punctuation and layout of the dialogue is correct, the children's writing makes a good class publication.

Differentiation

Less able
● Provide a checklist of editing points, which suggests what to look for at the start of the task.

More able
● Ask children to edit their work first and then consult the check list to see if they remembered all the points.

UNIT 1 HOUR 4 ▪ Narrative: perspective/character

Synonyms for *said*

Objectives

NLS
S2: To substitute pronouns for common and proper nouns.
W13: To collect synonyms which will be useful in writing dialogue.

What you need
● The children's work from Hour 3
● A4 paper, quartered to make pages for A6 books.

Shared word- and sentence-level work

● Tell the children that they will be editing the character conversations they wrote yesterday. Remind the class that pronouns can often be used in place of nouns, and that this helps the flow of the text. Write the following text on the board and model how to use pronouns in place of nouns and possessive pronouns where appropriate.

> Sidney had a new babysitter. They met at Sidney's house.
> 'What's your name,' said Jane to Sidney.
> 'It's Sidney,' Sidney said.
> 'Well, I've brought sweets. Would you like some?' said Jane.
> 'Yes please,' said Sidney. Jane dropped the sweets into Sidney's hand.
> 'Would you like to play this brand new PC game I happen to have on me?' said Jane. Jane showed Sidney a game Sidney had wanted to try for ages.

● Revise the need for synonyms for *said* and share children's suggestions from home. Record a long list on the board and include some in the text above.
● Suggest that it would be useful to have reference books of synonyms, categorised by emotion. Discuss useful headings, such as angry, happy, loving, sad, excited, frightened, playful.
● Explain to the children that they will need to think carefully about what each synonym implies about the emotions of the speaker. Depending on the categories chosen, some synonyms may need to be entered under more than one category. You may also want to have a 'catch-all' category for words that do not fit anywhere easily.

Guided and independent work

● Tell the children to write one category heading at the top of each section on an A4 sheet and construct their lists underneath.
● Now ask the children to cut up and staple the sheets to make an A6 booklet, with a title and their name on the front cover.
● Give children the opportunity to re-read the character conversations they wrote yesterday. Ask them to think about:

> ● whether they have sometimes used a noun where a pronoun would allow the text to 'flow' more appropriately
> ● whether the synonyms they used were most appropriate (If not, let them make changes using their booklets.)

● Ask the children to ensure that the punctuation and layout of the dialogue is correct before they are published as a class book.

Plenary

● Compare classifications. Did everyone make the same decisions? Which words were classified under several headings? Discuss words that were difficult to categorise.
● Talk about the editing. Were the synonym booklets useful?

Differentiation

Less able
● Suggest that children use fewer synonym headings, and ensure that they have at least some words under each heading when starting.
● Provide a poster reminder about pronouns and nouns.

More able
● Children will benefit from working with a greater number of synonym categories.

UNIT 1 HOUR 5 ▪ Narrative: perspective/character

First day at school

Shared text-level work

● Remind the children of how Charlotte's personality came through in her account of the football match. Elicit that it was not so much what she did but what she said about the events and other players that revealed what she was like.

● Explain to the children that they are going to write about their first day at school in a similar way. Before beginning, they will need to think about the sort of person they were when they started school. Choose a volunteer to help you to demonstrate this. Ask the children to briefly discuss in pairs the volunteer's best qualities. Then ask them to share these thoughts with the class for you to note on the board. Children will tend to talk about what the volunteer does and looks like, but encourage them to think beyond this, and consider personality traits and behaviours, such as kind, generous, friendly, fun, shy, intelligent.

● Continue this for different children, until you have a good list of personality traits and the children understand that they have to think beyond actions and appearances to understand characters in depth.

Guided and independent work

● Tell the children to think about their first day at school. Draw the table below on the board and ask the children to discuss the headings with a partner.

	My first journey to school	Arriving in the classroom	My first piece of work
What I heard others saying			
What I thought or said to myself			
What I said to others			

● Once the children have had an opportunity to recall and chat about this, ask them to talk about the differences between their memories, thoughts and reactions to their first days at school.

● Ask the children to write a three-paragraph, first-person narrative about their first day at school, based on the three headings provided in the table. The narrative should focus on their thoughts, feelings and relationships, including to whom they spoke and what they said and did.

● Encourage the children to read and discuss their accounts with their partners (or parents if you are running short of time) along these lines:

● Is the account interesting?
● Did any of it surprise you?
● What does it reveal about the author's personality and views?

Plenary

● Share the children's work and discuss how different people interpret and react to similar events in different ways.
● Do the children's accounts reflect their overall learning.

Talk Us Through It, Charlotte

Well I shouldn't've been playin' really
Only there to watch me brother.
My friend fancies his friend, y'know.
Anyway they was a man short.

Stay out on the wing, they said
Give 'em something to think about.
So I did that for about an hour;
Never passed to me or anything.

The ball kind of rebounded to me.
I thought, I'll have a little run with it.
I mean, they wasn't passin' to me
Was they? So off I went.

I ran past this first boy
He sort of fell over.
It was a bit slippery on that grass
I will say that for him.

Two more of 'em come at me
Only they sort of tackled each other
Collided - arh.* I kept going.
There was this great big fat boy.

One way or another I kicked it
Through his legs and run round him.
That took a time. Me brother
Was shouting, Pass it to me, like.

Well like I said, I'd been there an hour.
They never give me a pass
Never even spoke to me
Or anything. So I kept going.

Beat this other boy somehow
Then there was just the goalie.
Out he came, spreadin' himself
As they say. I was really worried.

I thought he was going to hug me.
So I dipped me shoulder like they do
And the goalie moved one way, y'know
And I slammed it in the net.

Turned out afterwards it was the winner.
The manager said I was very good.
He wants me down at trainin' on Tuesday.
My friend says she's comin' as well.

Allan Ahlberg

* Rhymes with 'car' – Charlotte's a Black Country girl.

Characters

Who meets whom?

Your teacher	An action figure doll	A pupil in your class	The Headteacher	Your mum
An old lady or old man	A cartoon character (your choice)	Cinderella	A wicked witch	Prince Charming
A thief	A pop star (your choice)	The Prime Minister	A rather smelly tramp	The Christmas Fairy

What are they doing?

Buying socks	Cooking a meal	Waiting for a late train	Trying to fix a broken-down car	Deciding where to go on holiday
Learning to skateboard	Looking around school	Complaining about service in a café	Arguing over the computer	Choosing hats to wear to a ball

UNIT 2

Narrative: plot

The unit is based on an adventure book and a scary story. Each offers a different way to explore narrative in terms of plot and setting, and there is some preparation work for the unit on characterisation, so it is suggested that this unit is done first.

The study of *Flat Stanley* by Jeff Brown (Egmont) will help children to appreciate good dialogue and effective beginnings. It is important that children are told at the beginning of the week that, by Friday, they will have written the first chapter of a book to be reviewed by their parents. The Flat Stanley Project at http://flatstanley.enorea.on.ca has information about Jeff Brown and the opportunity for children to post a paper Flat Stanley to each other and write his journal. This can provide a focus for further work and more details about the *Flat Stanley* series.

Week 2 explores how to write and tell a story. Children examine how John Prater creates the setting for a scary story in *Timid Tim and the Cuggy Thief* (Red Fox Books) They explore how to use dialogue to add atmosphere.

Where appropriate, encourage children to use homework time to re-read their stories, choose titles, design covers and illustrate their work, as well as read other books in the *Flat Stanley* series.

Hours 4 and 8 link to Unit 16 in *Grammar for Writing*; Hours 3 and 9 link to Unit 18.

Hour	Shared text-level work	Shared word-/ sentence-level work	Guided and independent work	Plenary
1 How it all began	Reading and discussing the opening of *Flat Stanley*; introducing the uses of dialogue.	Identifying dialogue and the use of speech marks.	Practising reading strategies; editing a text for dialogue layout and punctuation; creating own dialogue for the story.	Discussing correct speech and punctuation of speech; sharing new dialogues.
2 New sequels	Revising story structures, focusing on openings; sharing ideas for 'flat' situations.		Examining effective beginnings; writing two and choosing one as the basis of a new story.	Explaining choices and sharing new stories so far; thinking about the story overnight.
3 What happened next?	Discussing when/how it was helpful to think about the story, focusing on sequence of events.	Introducing time sequence words such as *first, then*.	Using either a talk planner or a visual planner to plan and write their stories.	Discussing chosen planners; sharing first drafts.
4 Editing		Editing a text for sense, spelling and style.	Suggesting edits for partner's work and then their own; considering where illustrations would be helpful.	Discussing likes, dislikes and editorial suggestions.
5 Visual literacy	Examining favourite pictures in stories; considering what illustrations add to a text and how they might be included in own stories.		Discussing choice of illustrations, before adding them and bringing stories to publication.	Displaying and reviewing stories, including with parents.

UNIT 2

Hour	Shared text-level work	Shared word-/ sentence-level work	Guided reading/ writing	Independent work	Plenary
6 Scary beginnings	Talking about known scary stories; reading and annotating a text to demonstrate how beginnings set atmosphere.		Oral descriptions of a darkened classroom; writing their own descriptions as the beginning of a scary story.	Read each other's beginnings in scary voices; noting developments from first oral draft.	Matching word cards to words on the board; Identifying sounds with various spellings.
7 The alien arrives	Identifying the initiating event in a story; sketching (planning) an alien character.		Writing this part of the story, including descriptions of characters and interactions.	Reading work in progress; discussing possible developments to consider overnight.	Sharing couplets; Focusing on long-vowel digraphs and rhymes.
8 Discovery dialogues	Developing their stories.	Revising speech marks; brainstorming synonyms for *said*.	Act out storyline and dialogue of discovery of the alien; writing this part of the story; commenting on each other's use of dialogue.	Collecting synonyms for *said*.	Reading and discussing new verses, focusing on rhyme.
9 The resolution	Discussing how illustrations help when creating a story; sketching pictorial events for own stories.	Discussing ways to join sentences and signal time sequences clearly; organising writing into paragraphs.	Using pictures and talk to sequence their stories and tell final parts; writing story endings.	Discussing which parts of the project were easy/hard; fun/less fun.	Discussing different uses of capital letters.
10 Celebrating the stories	Recapping on oral storytelling skills.		Practising telling their stories to themselves and to a friend; working on feedback issues and re-telling it to two others in the class; listening actively and evaluating.	Sharing one or two stories; discussing what has been learned about storytelling.	Sharing poems, focusing on spelling and discussing how punctuation affects reading.

Key assessment opportunities

- Can the children retell a story in sequence?
- Can they write effective story openings?
- Do they understand the use of speech marks?
- Can they read for meaning, using context visual and grammatical cues?
- Have the children enjoyed this enough to want to read more *Flat Stanley* books?
- Can the children write at length?

UNIT 2 HOUR 1 📖 **Narrative: plot**

How it all began

Objectives

NLS

T2: To refer to significant aspects of the text, eg opening, atmosphere.
T11: To write openings to stories or chapters linked to or arising from reading.
S1: To use awareness of grammar to decipher new or unfamiliar words.
S4: To use speech marks and other dialogue punctuation appropriately in writing.

What you need

● *Flat Stanley* by Jeff Brown
● photocopiable pages 153 and 154.

Differentiation

Less able
● Provide a list of two or three people Flat Stanley meets (a teacher worried about how he will sit on the chairs; a snooty parent who thinks he should be expelled; a concerned classroom assistant; bullying children; supportive children...). Speech bubbles may help with writing.

More able
● Suggest that the dialogue should suggest characters' personalities.

Shared text-level work

● Introduce *Flat Stanley* to the children and read the first two pages to them, emphasising the different speakers by putting on different character voices.
● Explain that dialogue at the beginning of a story can tell us about the characters and help to set the atmosphere for the story. Ask the children what they imagine Mr and Mrs Lambchop are like, and why. Would their own parents react like Mr and Mrs Lambchop? What would they say? What about Stanley's reaction? Would the children have reacted as cheerfully?

Shared sentence-level work

● Prepare the children for group work on dialogue. Use photocopiable page 153 to show how the dialogue in *Flat Stanley* is identified and set out. Ask the children to help you to annotate the text to show that speech marks open and close the spoken words, and a new line indicates a new speaker.
● Ask the children to suggest why it is helpful for readers to have dialogue clearly indicated.

Guided and independent work

● Read photocopiable page 154 with the children. Demonstrate how to use reading strategies to decipher unfamiliar words. For example, *examination* might need to be broken into syllables; other words such as *finished* might be read from the context.
● Ask the children to read the text aloud quietly to themselves, using different character voices, and then mark where they think speech marks and new lines should go. Visual learners should mark their texts in a coloured 'editing pen'.
● Then ask the children to compare their edit with their writing partners', marking any uncertain or 'disputed' areas of text for discussion during the plenary.
● Explain to the children that they will be writing about what happens the next day, when Flat Stanley goes to school. Consider: Who does he meet when he first arrives? What do the teachers, other children or the headteacher say to him? What do they say to each other?
● Ask the children to begin their story by writing this dialogue between Flat Stanley and the people he meets. Encourage them to work through the dialogue orally in pairs before writing it down.

Plenary

● How accurate were the children in marking-up the dialogue? Identify and discuss common difficulties.
● Ask some children to read their dialogues of Flat Stanley at school, using their voices to indicate characterisation. The children can complete these stories as a homework task.
● Finish the session by reading all or part of *Flat Stanley* to the class.

UNIT 2 HOUR 2 Narrative: plot

New sequels

Objectives

NLS
T2: To refer to significant aspects of the text (opening, build up, atmosphere).
T4: To consider credibility of events.
W6: To use independent spelling strategies.

What you need
- *Flat Stanley*
- photocopiable page 154.

Shared text-level work
- Explain to the children that they will be writing sequels to *Flat Stanley*. Remind them that stories need characters, a setting, and an event or problem to start the story off.
- The children are now familiar with the characters but ask them to brainstorm, in pairs, ideas for the settings given at the top of the photocopiable sheet. Explain that any of these could be an initiating event for a *Flat Stanley* story. Discuss the setting ideas before asking the children to select one for their own story.
- Read the beginning of *Flat Stanley* to show how it has both pace and detail to make it interesting. Demonstrate how details can make a beginning effective.

Guided and independent work
- Ask the children to read part B of the photocopiable sheet and annotate the beginnings to identify two things that make each effective. For example, the huge crash literally crashes into the quiet, serene setting; the repetition of *happy-go-lucky* and *bright side* sets the story up for a life-changing event very much of the opposite nature.
- Encourage the children to explain to their writing partners which parts they identified, and why. If appropriate, take brief feedback on this as a whole class.
- Read part C of the sheet and explain how a story can begin.
- Ask the children to choose two different starting points and use them to write two short beginnings for their own 'Flat Stanley' adventure. Remind them to include details to make each of their beginnings effective and believable. Ask them to check their spellings of new words.
- Now tell the children to read each of their beginnings, choose one and think about how the story will continue. Encourage them to make a few notes on this.
- Help visual learners by explaining that writers often imagine the beginning of a story as if it were a film. Tell them to close their eyes and visualise the opening shots. Verbal learners should read aloud or discuss their openings with their partner to choose the best.

Differentiation

Less able
- Work on the photocopiable sheet in pairs or as a teacher-led activity.
- Provide a writing frame for the story beginnings.

More able
- Children should try to use more sophisticated grammatical strategies, such as repetition, to set the scene.

Plenary
- Ask the children to share their beginnings and explain their choices. Discuss why they are effective. Discuss the favourite beginning from part B if you have not already done so.
- Finally, explain that they will continue their story tomorrow but should think about it overnight.
- Suggest that they may get good ideas by talking to a friend, parent or sibling; relaxing; drawing, playing or acting out the story with toys.

What happened next?

Objectives

NLS

T1: To retell main points of a story in sequence; to evaluate stories and justify their preferences.

T10: To plot a sequence of episodes, modelled on a known story, as a plan for writing.

S6: To investigate through reading and writing how words and phrases can signal time sequences.

S&L

28 Drama: To present events and characters through dialogue.

Shared text-level work

● Discuss the homework from Hour 2 and where, when and how the children thought about the rest of their story.

● Explain that writers like different atmospheres when they are writing. Some like noise, with the television or music on in the background, but others like it to be very quiet. They also plan their stories in different ways. Some like to draw, others to talk; some like peace and quiet to think on their own. Some do not know the whole story before they begin, just a rough outline, and think of the details as they write.

● Ask the children to share their own preferences and then offer them a choice of the following two ways to plan: they can either draw key events for the rest of their story, or jot down a few 'bare bones' to use as a basis for telling the rest of their story orally to a partner.

Shared sentence-level work

● Remind the children that, to make the story sequence clear, authors use words and phrases such as *first, then, after, meanwhile, from* and *where*. Display these where the children can refer to them while writing, and suggest that they think about them as they plan. They may also think about strong verbs and interesting descriptive language and phrases that they might use when writing their story. Encourage them to jot these down if they fear they may not remember them when it comes to writing.

Guided and independent work

● Separate the class so that the 'drawers' can do this in relative peace and the 'talkers' are sitting together. Allow about fifteen minutes for the children to plan the rest of their story.

● You may need to remind the talkers at half time to ensure that both partners get a reasonable chance to talk through their story. You may also need to check that the drawers are mapping out all the key events, rather than producing one, very detailed illustration.

● Then let the children use their plans to write their stories.

Plenary

● Discuss as a whole class what the children thought of the planning mechanism they tried. Did it suit them? Would they like to try something different next time?

● Set up a storyteller's chair and ask children to share their stories so far. (Any unfinished stories should be completed for homework.) Invite comments on the samples of work read out. For each piece of work, ask the children to suggest one good thing and one thing that, if the story were theirs, they might change. Encourage them to think about story ideas and language.

Differentiation

Less able

● Encourage children to verbalise their thoughts. Help non-intrusively by modelling and scribing key phrases.

More able

● Encourage independence and reflection on what they have written.

UNIT 2 HOUR 4 ■ Narrative: plot

Editing

Objectives

NLS
S4: To use speech marks and other dialogue punctuation appropriately in writing.
W5: To identify mis-spelt words in their own writing.
W6: To use independent spelling strategies.

What you need
● Text to be edited (if appropriate, the first part of long stories written by confident children)
● the children's stories from Hour 3
● green editing pens.

Shared word- and sentence-level work
● Remind the children that an editor checks that writing is clear and makes sense, and improves it by checking spelling and style. Explain that, like other skills, editing skills develop with practise
● Show the text to be edited. Model how to read and edit the text for clarity, spelling, punctuation and use of language. Explain that these features all help the reader to understand what the writer wants to say and to enjoy the text.
● Finally, discuss appropriate places and subjects for illustrations.

Guided and independent work
● Organise the children into pairs. Ask them to read their partner's story to identify where it may need editing (they should mark the text lightly in pencil to suggest changes in the margin or by underlining mis-spelt words), but not to make the changes. Display this list to remind the editors of what to do:

● Identify any parts that are unclear.
● Underline words that are mis-spelled.
● Check for correct use of full stops, capital letters, speech marks, question marks, exclamation marks.
● Identify a verb that might be replaced by a stronger, more expressive word.
● Identify one good place and a subject for an illustration.

● Give the children a brief opportunity to talk about what they have noticed in their partner's work and to make helpful suggestions. (You may want to explain that editors and authors do not always agree about what needs to be changed!) Encourage the partners to each identify one (or more) particular area on the editing list that they think the author is good at, and one area for further thought and attention.
● Afterwards, ask the pairs to swap roles.
● Tell each author to use a green editing pen to make any changes. Let the children edit their stories and indicate with an asterisk one or two places where they would like to include illustrations.
● Circulate to ensure that the children are acting on key editing points.

Plenary
● Discuss the following:

● what children liked about their partners' stories
● changes suggested, and why
● changes that were made, and why.

● Ask the children to comment on which aspects of editing they found the easiest or most difficult.
● Finally talk about where the children chose to illustrate their story. Explain that they will think about illustrations in more detail next time. In the meantime, ask the children to collect a good example in a fiction book and be prepared to talk about it.

Differentiation

Less able
● Allocate yourself as a writing partner or ensure that you have seen the editing decisions children are making.

More able
● Encourage children to add a short illustration brief with their edit.

UNIT 2 HOUR 5 📖 Narrative: plot

Visual literacy

Objectives

NLS
T1: To evaluate stories and justify their preferences.
T2: To refer to significant aspects of the text.
W17: To practise correct formation of basic joins and use these for independent writing.

What you need

● Story books collected by the children
● different shapes and sizes of paper
● art and craft materials
● computer access (optional).

Shared text-level work

● Explain to the children that they are going to illustrate and publish their books and so need to think about the role of pictures in their story.
● Talk about the illustrations they have brought with them and why they chose them. What makes them effective? This will raise issues about quality, style and content. It may also raise points about the size, shape and position of illustrations, and their function within the story.
● Discuss how illustrations often add detail to the story and give us more information about the plot, characters and setting.
● Show the paper shapes available for illustrations and give tips to ensure that the children's illustrations have a strong impact. You might mention colouring the background to make an illustration look 'finished'; that colouring right up to the edge makes a clear border whereas background colours that fade towards the edge 'blend' the illustration into text. Note how selective use of glitter or coloured gel pens can create striking effects.

Guided and independent work

● Encourage the children to talk briefly with partners about the illustrations in the books they brought along. How are they used and what makes them effective?
● Ask the children to explain to each other the illustrations they plan to put in their stories.
● The stories can now be published as a handwritten book (encouraging correct formation of basic joins), or as an ICT project.
● Before publishing, suggest that the children read their text aloud (either to their partner or themselves) to check that they are happy with the edited version and that the punctuation guides the reader by indicating pauses, intonation and dialogue.
● Suggest that some writers may like to write out the whole text first, simply choosing the size and shape of paper to use for illustrations to ensure that they leave appropriate spaces. Others may prefer to do the illustrations as they go, using drawing to provide a legitimate break from the writing task. For children who are publishing on computer, illustrations may be scanned in and placed appropriately.

Plenary

● Display the children's work. Point out attractive layout, effective illustration and powerful writing.
● Ask the children to finish their stories as homework if necessary.
● What do the children feel they have learned from this unit so far? Invite individuals to contribute a sentence to a class poster. Copies can be sent home for discussion with parents.
● Ask parents and carers to read and respond to their child's story. Provide review sheets that will help them to structure their feedback.

Differentiation

Less able
● Ensure that you spend time explaining what you admire in their story, and why it is a good read.

More able
● Encourage children to do this for each other, as well as for less able children in the class.

Scary beginnings

Objectives

NLS
T2: To refer to significant aspects of the text, eg atmosphere, and to know language is used to create these.
T11: To write openings to stories linked to or arising from reading; to focus on language to create effects, eg suspense, creating moods, setting scenes.

S&L
29 Speaking: To prepare stories for performance, identifying appropriate expression, tone, volume and use of voices.

What you need
● Photocopiable page 156.

Shared text-level work
● Talk about any scary stories that the children have previously read and enjoyed.
● Use examples to explain that sometimes stories are scary because of the characters, and sometimes because of the setting. Descriptions of spooky noises, smells and textures help to make a setting eerie. Film-makers frighten people with scary images and music, but authors have a harder task because they use only words. Describing spooky noises, smells and textures help to make a text scary. Explain to the children that they will learn to write and tell their own scary stories.
● Read the extract on photocopiable page 156. Ask groups to annotate the text to identify the phrases and words that make it scary before discussing this as a class. Talk about the build up of suspense too.

Guided and independent work
● Explain to the children that they are going to write a scary story set in a darkened classroom after school. Ask the children to imagine the scene, and brainstorm scary words and phrases. Think about the scene in terms of all the senses – hearing, smell and touch as well as sight.
● Organise the children into pairs and label each child either A or B. Give the children labelled A one minute to describe the picture to their partner's, making their description as scary as possible, both in their choice of vocabulary and tone and pace of voice. Then ask the children labelled B to do the same.
● Now tell all the A children to remain sitting and ask the B children to move and find a new A partner. Give the new partners one minute each to describe their scary classroom to each other. Then tell the A pupils to stand and find new B partners and retell their scary settings.
● Expect this part of the lesson to be fairly noisy! To re-focus the children, explain that this talking session acts as a planning strategy for writing; that listening to others expands vocabulary and exposes the children to a range of models.
● Now ask the children to write a scary story beginning by describing the classroom at night. Encourage them to make their beginnings as detailed as possible.

Plenary
● Ask the children to read their writing to the first partner with whom they worked. Give them the opportunity to read each other's beginnings aloud in suitably scary voices. Once they have had a chance to rehearse this, select some to read to the class.
● Ask the children to comment on the differences between this final, written description and the first oral description they heard.

Differentiation

Less able
● Encourage children to fix the image of the scene in their mind before they begin talking.

More able
● Ask children to work with partners outside their normal friendship group.

The alien arrives

Objectives

NLS
T13: To write more extended stories based on a plan of incidents.
W6: To use independent spelling strategies.

What you need
● Photocopiable page 156
● the children's story beginnings from Hour 6.

Shared text-level work
● Remind the children of the scary openings they created in Hour 6. Explain that authors make key decisions about characters and initiating events to drive the plot on from this beginning.
● Re-read the beginning of photocopiable page 156. Help the children to see that the cuggy being stolen is the initiating event in the story.
● Suggest an initiating event for the children's scary stories: A young alien has accidentally transported itself into their darkened classroom. It is lonely and scared.
● Ask the children to do a quick, rough sketch (taking just a few minutes) of their alien. Explain that this will help their storytelling and need not be a work of art.
● Put the children in mixed-ability groups of three, and ask them to show and describe their alien sketches to each other.
● Ask the children to brainstorm specific language to describe how their own alien shows fear, what it thinks or says; what scares it most, and what it does. For example, their alien might turn a different colour when frightened or speak a strange alien language.
● Ask the children to close their eyes and imagine their story so far as a film. It begins with a darkened classroom. Where exactly in the classroom does their alien land? How does it react to being in the classroom and what might it do?

Guided and independent work
● Ask the children to write the initiating part of their story - the alien landing in their classroom.
● Tell the children to use the ideas they brainstormed earlier. Explain that as storytellers, they must be very careful to describe what the alien looks like, how it feels, what it thinks to itself and what it does to show that it is lonely and scared. Explain that they should try to write in a way that will let their readers imagine the scene in their heads.
● Encourage them to use independent spelling strategies and to re-read their work, listening to what their story sounds like.

Plenary
● Ask some children tell or read their stories so far to the class (using their work both from yesterday and today).
● Discuss ideas for the final two sections of the story - how the alien is discovered and what happens in the end.
● Ask the children to think overnight about ideas for the rest of their story. Remind them of how they got ideas for *Flat Stanley* and suggest that telling their story so far at home may also be helpful.

Differentiation

Less able
● Encourage children to talk during the writing process. This will help them to generate ideas.

More able
● Encourage children to re-read and revise their work independently.

Discovery dialogues

Objectives

NLS
T13: To write more extended stories based on a plan of incidents.
S4: To use speech marks and other dialogue punctuation appropriately in writing.
W13: To collect synonyms which will be useful in writing dialogue.

S&L
36 Drama: To use some drama strategies to explore stories.

What you need
● Story books containing examples of dialogue.

Shared text-level work
● Write these story prompts on the board before the lesson:

> ● Who discovers your alien? Why are they late in the school? (A policeman notices movement when walking past? Teachers working late? Caretaker or cleaners...?)
> ● How do they first notice it? (A movement? Noise? Displaced furniture?)
> ● What do they first say to themselves? To others?
> ● What do they say to the alien? What does it say to them?

● Remind the children that stories need an opening, an initiating event, a development and a resolution. Explain that they already have written the opening and initiating events for their stories and today will write the development: who discovers the alien and how they react.

Shared word- and sentence-level work
● Draw attention to the headings on the board, outlining the decisions the children will need to make. Explain that this part of the story will also include some dialogue.
● Ask what they already know about writing dialogue, for example, how speech marks help the reader. Remind them that repetition of *said* can get boring and alternative words, such as *shouted, cried, wept* and *whimpered*, will add to the atmosphere because they indicate how words were said and so the emotional state of the speaker. Tell the children to refer to the resource booklets they made in the first half of this unit.
● Distribute the books and ask the children to find examples of dialogue that illustrate some of the points discussed. Use these to consolidate understandings and to prompt further discussion.

Guided and independent work
● Ask the children to use the prompt questions on the board to decide how their alien is discovered, by whom and what is said.
● Develop this into a mini drama lesson, with the children in pairs acting out the discovery of each other's alien monsters.
● Once you feel that this part of the storyline is clear, and the dialogue thought through, ask the children to write this part of the story. Remind them that dialogue must be clear and effective, with synonyms for *said* used where appropriate to conjure lively images in the reader's mind.
● Ask the children to check that their writing partner's dialogue is easy to read (indicated by speech marks, each new speaker on a new line, and that it is clear who is speaking) and to find at least one good example of a synonym for *said* to discuss in the plenary.

Plenary
● Ask the children to share well-chosen synonyms for *said*.
● Announce a homework competition to collect as many synonyms for *said* as possible.

Differentiation

Less able
● Encourage children to re-read as they write and to read their story with expression so that they develop an 'ear' for their writing, or read it aloud for them.

More able
● Encourage children to engage in this re-reading spontaneously for themselves, listening to what their story might sound like to a reader.

The resolution

Objectives

NLS
T2: To refer to significant aspects of the text.
S6: To investigate through reading and writing how words and phrases can signal time sequences.

What you need

● Well-illustrated books such as those by Babette Cole and Frank Rodgers
● the children's stories.

Shared text-level work

● Before the lesson, write a list of temporal and spatial connectives on the board: *first, then, after, meanwhile, from, where* and so on.
● Remind the children about how the process of creating their alien stories began – with a picture of a darkened classroom. Discuss how examination of the picture inspired and helped to focus their ideas for talking and writing.
● Explain that authors such as Babette Cole and Frank Rodgers draw pictures throughout the writing process to help them to imagine and plan their stories.
● Explain to the children that they are now going to craft the resolution to their stories – how their stories end by sketching two pictures. The first should show what happens to their alien. Does it get home? How? Perhaps it stays happily on earth? The second should show how other characters in the story feel about what happens to the alien. Stress that, as before the drawings do not have to be perfect, but serve as an important planning device. Whilst the children draw, they should be thinking about their storyline and how they will write it.

Shared sentence-level work

● Explain that to keep stories interesting and clear for listeners or readers, it is important to use phrases to indicate time and sequence. Show the list on the board and suggest how the children can use them.
● Remind the children that chunking their ideas into paragraphs can make writing more accessible and help the reader to get a better understanding of the story. Each paragraph should detail a separate incident in the story.

Guided and independent work

● As the children quickly draw, talk to individuals, asking them to explain what happens at the end of their story. Reflect what these children say back to them and model appropriate use of a range of connectives and time sequence words whilst you talk.
● Organise the children into pairs and encourage them to talk in as much detail as possible about their pictures and to use them to tell the final part of their story to their partners.
● Ask the children to write their story endings.

Differentiation

Less able
● While the children are drawing, talk with those children who have difficulty in generating ideas or in finding the words to describe what happens.

More able
● Encourage children to use the drawing session to generate ideas for themselves and to jot down good words and phrases as they draw.

Plenary

● What did the children feel about writing their stories this week? Which parts of the work were easy, which were hard? Which were good fun and which did they not enjoy so much?
● Say that tomorrow they will tell their stories, and get evaluations of them. Tonight, they should read them through and practise reading or telling them orally.

UNIT 2 HOUR 10 ▢ Narrative: plot

Celebrating the stories

Objectives

NLS

T1: To retell the main points of a story in sequence; to evaluate stories and justify their preferences.
T2: To refer to significant aspects of the text and to know language is used to create these.

S&L

18 Listening: To respond to presentations by repeating some highlights and commenting constructively.
29 Speaking: To prepare stories for performance.
32 Drama: To identify and discuss qualities of others' performances.

What you need
● The children's stories.

Shared text-level work
● Remind the children of the importance of telling their stories effectively to keep listeners' attention and interest. Recap on the performance skills learned during last term's poetry reading festival. Use this discussion to generate a list of good points to consider when reading aloud, for example:

● a good introduction
● speaking clearly and loudly (but not shouting!)
● eye contact with the listener
● varying the tone and quality of voice for different parts of the performance
● confident body language.

● Ask the children to suggest additional factors, specific to storytelling, such as:

● use of descriptive language
● use of different voices for each character's speech
● clear indication of the sequence of events.

Guided and independent work
● Give the children an opportunity to prepare and practise reading or telling their stories aloud to themselves.
● Then ask them to work with a friend and to listen to each other's stories. Tell the listeners to provide feedback on the storyline (particularly any sections that are not clear) and the quality of story language, as well as success in the storytelling skills listed on the board. They should state what they liked about the performance and one aspect that needs further practise.
● Provide time and support for the writers to improve the aspects identified by their audiences.
● Now organise the children into mixed-ability groups of three and ask them to introduce and tell their stories to each other.
● At the end of each performance, the two listeners should each retell the story in their own words and write down or explain one good thing about the story and one good thing about they way in which it was told.
● Explain that you are interested in these responses, not only because they provide an evaluation of the stories, but also because they indicate the quality of the telling and listening. You will therefore be judging the quality of evaluative comments as a reflection of listening skills.

Plenary
● Select one or two confident children to tell their stories to the whole class. Briefly take comments on them from the class.
● End the lesson by discussing the children's evaluative comments. Talk about what has been learned in this unit about writing, crafting stories and storytelling.
● If possible, arrange for children to tell their stories to another class.

Differentiation

Less able
● Ensure that children are in supportive groups that will help them to take the task seriously, and to identify and explain what makes the story good.

More able
● Ensure that children develop their listening and evaluation skills, and do not dominate.

Dialogue in Flat Stanley

■ Write you own annotations to explain how the dialogue in *Flat Stanley* has been identified and set out.

But Stanley was not hurt. In fact he would still have been sleeping if he had not been woken by his brother's shout.

"What's going on here?" he called out cheerfully from beneath the enormous board. Mr and Mrs Lambchop hurried to lift it from the bed.

"Heavens!" said Mrs Lambchop.

"Gosh!" said Arthur. "Stanley's flat!"

"As a pancake," said Mr Lambchop.

"Darndest thing I've ever seen."

"Let's all have breakfast," Mrs Lambchop said. "Then Stanley and I will go and see Doctor Dan and hear what he has to say."

Jeff Brown

TERM 3

Editing dialogue

◼ Read the first paragraph. Add speech marks and mark new paragraphs to help the reader understand who is speaking. Compare your answers with a friend. Put a star beside any parts where you do not agree.

The examination was almost over. How do you feel? Doctor Dan asked. Does it hurt very much? I felt sort of tickly for a while after I got up, Stanley Lambchop said, but I feel fine now. Well that's mostly how it is with these cases said Doctor Dan. We'll just have to keep an eye on this young fellow, he said when he had finished the examination. Sometimes we doctors, despite all our years of training and experience, can only marvel at how little we really know.

Mrs Lambchop said she thought that Stanley's clothes would have to be altered by the tailor now, so Doctor Dan told his nurse to take Stanley's measurements.

Mrs Lambchop wrote them down.

Stanley was four feet tall, about a foot wide and half an inch thick.

Jeff Brown

Settings for Flat Stanley

Part A

◼ Think of two good and two bad things about being flat in each of the following places:

- School
- The supermarket
- The cinema
- Playing outside

Part B

◼ What makes each of the following beginnings effective? Which do you think is best? Why?

1. The room was dark. David Martin was safe in bed, fast asleep. He was dreaming happy, peaceful dreams. You could tell his dreams were happy and peaceful because he smiled as he slept in his big, solid bed.

CRASH! The huge shelf above the bed fell off the wall and landed on the sleeping boy. It was a big wooden shelf, with big heavy books. It covered the whole of David and nearly covered the whole of David's bed. It was so heavy that David, who had suddenly woken up, found that he was pinned down. Stuck. He couldn't move...

2. David Martin was a happy-go-lucky boy. He came from a happy-go-lucky family. Whenever terrible things happened, Mr and Mrs Martin and their children, David and Rebecca, all tried, as hard as they could, to look on the bright side. And when they looked, they found that there usually *was* a bright side, and it usually *was* worth looking on.

This approach to life worked well until David Martin was eight years old. Then, something happened that changed his life for ever...

Part C

◼ Here are some ways that stories can begin:

- With a conversation
- By describing a scene
- By describing an action or event
- By describing a character.

Timid Tim and the Cuggy Thief

◼ Tim is shy and he does not like noisy, messy games. He loves his cuggy, a special comfort blanket that he cuddles at night.

One dark and windy night Tim lay in bed, holding his cuggy tight. But when he fell asleep, he tossed and turned - and let it go! A chilling blast of air blew through the bedroom, and Tim awoke to find his cuggy gone.

The setting is scary. It is windy.

Contrast with Tim safe asleep in bed.

Chilling blast - icy air always makes you think something horrible is going to happen, or someone horrible has arrived

He let out a little cry which grew bigger, and bigger and bigger... until he yelled at the top of his voice, "Come back you thief! You rascal! give me back my cuggy!" Tim leapt out into the night to catch the thief.

Scary, tense feeling as Tim chases the thief

The streets were dark and empty. The wood was darker still. The path was steep, the mud was deep, and though his heart beat fast, Tim never took his eyes off the wicked rogue ahead. The weather grew wild and the waves crashed loud. But Tim bravely kept going on.

John Prater

Dark and nightime are scary

Empty streets mean that noone will be around to help

The steep path is dangerous and he may slip or get stuck in the mud

The wood is scary – monsters and witches might hide there

Wild weather and scary, uncontrolled sea make you realise Tim is alone.

UNIT 3 🔲

Poetry

In this unit the children prepare a poetry wall of different kinds of humorous poem. The organisation of the poetry wall (one section per day) will emphasise the forms of humour in poetry. The children will discuss, choose and illustrate the poems for each section. In addition, they should choose poems from this unit to add to their poetry anthologies started in Term 1. The children are also encouraged to perform some of the poems for their parents or visitors to the class.

The poems on display will be a mixture of those written by professional poets and by the children themselves. The children can use ICT to prepare their poems but this work can provide a meaningful context for handwriting practice.

Hour	Shared text-level work	Shared word-/ sentence-level work	Guided and independent work	Plenary
1 Limericks	Revising rhythm and rhyme of limericks.		Sorting out jumbled-up limericks; writing own limerick.	Sharing limericks; taking home for parents; choosing some for poetry wall.
2 Pizza poetry	Writing a class list poem about a pizza.		Redrafting the lines of the poem to personalise; writing own poem about food.	Sharing poems and discussing the humour; adding to poetry wall.
3 Funny stories and cautionary tales	Understanding longer poems; dramatic recitations of story poem.	Identifying problematic words.	Working on reciting/reading a poem as performance; writing an introduction for it.	Introducing and performing poetry; performing for parents; adding to poetry wall.
4 Playing with words and sounds	Identifying the different ways that poems can play with words and sounds.	Analysing tongue twisters, homonyms and homophones.	Writing alliterative poems based on own names; making 'Knock-knock' jokes into poetry.	Sequencing the alliterative poem lines to make a class poem; discussing other choices.
5 Football and other favourites	Performing a football poem; discussing humour and explaining preferences.		Writing and performing new verses for football poem; choosing and memorising another poem.	Combining to perform poem as a class; discussing choices; completing poetry wall.

Key assessment opportunities
● Do the children read poetry with expression and meaning?
● Can they choose and talk about favourite poems?
● Do they recognise how rhythm, rhyme and layout affect the way poems are read?
● Can they explain different types of funny poem, and why they are different?

Limericks

Objectives

NLS

T7: To select, prepare, read aloud and recite by heart poetry that plays with language or entertains; to recognise rhyme and other patterns of sound.
T15: To write poetry that uses sound to create effects, eg distinctive rhythms.
W17: To practise correct formation of basic joins.
W19: To build up handwriting speed, fluency and legibility through practice.

What you need
● Photocopiable page 163
● a copy of *The Beano*
● other limericks to display.

Shared text-level work
● Show the children some limericks, and ask them to join in reading them aloud as a whole class.
● Check that the children remember that these poems are called limericks and can explain their distinctive rhythm and rhyme.
● Revise this rhythm by asking the children to recite each line using nonsense words (such as *diddle de diddle de de...*).
● Give extra familiarity with the rhythm by getting the children to repeat these 'nonsense limericks' in pairs to each other and again with the whole class. This time, however, ask one child to *diddle de de* the first line, another to continue with the second, another with the third line and so on.
● Revise the rhyme scheme(s) by asking the children to identify the rhyming lines in the limericks that you read together at the beginning of the lesson.
● If possible, show a copy of the 'Rhyme Time' page from *The Beano* comic and read some of the limericks contributed by readers. Suggest that children might like to send some of their own work in for publication on the 'Rhyme Time' page.

Guided and independent work
● Show the children that the lines of the limericks on the photocopiable sheet have been muddled up. Ask the children to sort them out by numbering the correct sequence of lines. Explain that the first limericks are simple muddles, with their lines in the wrong order. The second one is more complicated as it combines lines from two different limericks.
● Finally, ask the children to have a go at writing their own limerick, using the starter lines provided on the photocopiable sheet. Remind them of the rhythm and rhymes they have previously explored.
● Advise the children that some of the poems will be displayed on the poetry wall and give them time to copy out their limerick in best handwriting (ensuring correct formation of basic joins), or using the computer, whichever is appropriate.

Plenary
● Check that the children have sequenced the lines correctly, by encouraging some to read the limericks aloud.
● Share some of the children's own limericks.
● Tell the children to take all the limericks home (including those they have written themselves) to read or recite to their parents.
● Ask the children to ask their parents if they know of any good limericks for the poetry wall, children should bring these to school.
● Help the children to choose a selection of limericks for the poetry wall, explaining what they specifically like about each choice.

Differentiation

Less able
● Ask children to complete part A alone. You should be prepared to offer adult support to discuss and complete B and C if necessary.

More able
● Ask children to complete the whole sheet without any assistance.

Pizza poetry

Objectives

NLS
T6: To compare forms or types of humour.
T21: To use IT to bring to a published form – discuss relevance of layout, font, etc.

What you need
● Photograph of a pizza (from an advert or box).

Shared text-level work

● Explain that somewhat odd, insignificant topics can make for funny poems. Robert Burns once wrote a poem about a head louse crawling on a woman's hair! Famously, he also wrote an ode to a haggis, which is recited by his fans each Burns Night.

● Show the children the photograph and say that you are going to write a class list poem about pizza. Ask them to name four things they can see in the picture. Write these as a list down the middle of the board. Then ask for a description of each item. Write these to the left, beginning each line with a capital letter. Take each line in turn and ask the class to suggest how to finish it off. For example:

> Lovely dripping cheese, looking just right to eat
> Red tomato sauce, tangy and glistening
> Crispy crust, straight from the oven
> Sweet yellow pineapple, saying, 'Eat me now'.

Guided and independent work

● Ask the children to work in pairs to reorder the lines and allow them to change two lines they do not like. Finally, ask them to add another line, anywhere they choose.

● Hold a brief feedback session to explore the decisions made. Emphasise that there is no right answer, but the reasons underlying the decisions are interesting and important.

● Now tell the class that they are going to write another list poem about food, this time about the most horrible sandwich in the world! Have fun brainstorming the worst, most disgusting, outlandish sandwich fillings possible.

● Ask the children to work individually to write four lines for a poem about a horrible sandwich. Each line should detail one filling, saying what it is, and describing what it is like. The children may use ideas from the brainstorm, or invent their own.

● Then, ask pairs of children to pool their lines but work individually to combine them, making an eight line poem each. They should redraft any lines that need changing.

● Once finished, ask the groups to compare their poems, noting that they all had the same starting point.

● If appropriate, the, children could publish their poems using ICT, choosing an appropriate layout and font.

Plenary

● Discuss the poems the children created and the decisions they made. Discuss what makes them funny and entertaining.

● Choose some poems for the poetry wall. When choosing, the children should consider the content of the poems and also look for particularly interesting layout and attractive presentation.

Differentiation

Less able
● Children may be motivated by using ICT to produce the final poems.

More able
● Children should be encouraged to explain the reasons for their changes, and consider alternative changes and reasons.

UNIT 3 HOUR 3 🔲 Poetry

Funny stories and cautionary tales

Objectives

NLS
T6: To compare forms or types of humour.
T7: To select, prepare, read aloud and recite by heart poetry that plays with language or entertains.
S1: To use awareness of grammar to decipher new or unfamiliar words.

S&L
29 Speaking: To choose and prepare poems for performance, identifying appropriate expression, tone, volume and use of voices.

What you need

● Photocopiable pages 164–166.

Differentiation

Less able
● Children may benefit from working from slightly shorter poems, or in a group with adult support.

More able
● Encourage more able children to select more difficult and longer poems.

Shared text- and sentence-level work
● Tell the children that some poems are written to tell funny stories. They are often longer than other poems and may need to be read several times, once for the story and again to appreciate the rhymes and characterisation.
● Explain that the poems that they are going to read in this lesson are also stories. Some are cautionary tales, which warn of the terrible things that happen to bad children!
● Introduce your choice of first poem as you would a story (identifying the main character and the problem they face, but not revealing the ending). Say what you like about the poem, and talk about the writer.
● Ask the children to read the poem in pairs, reminding them of reading strategies to use on unfamiliar words. Ask the children to circle anything they do not understand. Discuss these before helping them recap the main events and message of the poem.
● Explain that the poem should be recited with as much drama as possible. Model how to read part of the poem dramatically, before letting the children read alternate verses to their partners.

Guided and independent work
● Ask the children to read the remaining poems in pairs and choose one to perform. They should take it in turns to read verses of the poem. Ask them to try to figure out together anything they do not understand, before asking you.
● Tell the children to decide together how they will read their chosen poem. Encourage them to annotate their copies to remind them about actions, tone of voice, pace and so on. Remind them that they are telling a story.
● Now ask the children to write a short introduction for their poem. This should stimulate the listeners' interest by saying who the poem is about and the problem (but not what happens), who wrote it and why they have chosen to perform it.

Plenary
● Ask the children to introduce and perform their chosen poems. Did they spot the cautionary tales? What were they cautioning against? Praise effective readings and good introductions.
● Discuss any parts that the children did not understand at first and how they worked them out.
● For homework, ask the children to practise and perform their poem on different occasions outside school. In addition, or alternatively, ask the children to illustrate their favourite part of the poem.
● Finally, ask the children which poems they think should go on the wall display, and why.

Playing with words and sounds

Shared text-level work

● Begin by reading 'An attempt at unrhymed verse' by Wendy Cope. Remind the children that humorous poetry often plays with sounds. Rhyming is only one way of doing this. Show and read 'The Tutor'. This rhymes, but also uses alliteration and long vowel sounds that are funny and difficult to say. Let the children read the poem slowly and identify the difficulties. What confuses them?
● Have fun with the poem, reciting it as a class, then as a class race or in pairs, racing their partners.

Shared word-level work

● Now read and discuss 'A Fly and a Flea'. Explain what a flue is.
● This poem is also difficult to say quickly but has an added dimension in that some words are homophones and some homonyms. Help the children to identify these and discuss the humour.
● Examine other alliterative tongue-twisters such as *Peter Piper picked a peck of pickled pepper* and *She sells sea shells...* These could be considered as poems. So too could 'Knock-knock' jokes. Ask the children to share some that they know.

Guided and independent work

● Explain to the children that they are going to make lines for a class poem based on their names. Ask them to help each other write one alliterative line of poetry using their first names (like the 'Peter Piper' poem). They should copy this onto the paper strips, using layout and lettering to indicate how they want it read. Remind them that you will be asking them to explain why they have used capital letters, different letter sizes, spacing and punctuation to make the reader read their alliterative poems in a particular way.
● Ask the children to brainstorm 'Knock-knock' jokes and choose one for the poetry display. They should consider how to present their joke as poetry, thinking about the pattern of the words and where the line breaks need to come.
● Finally, give the children poetry anthologies and ask them to find other poems that play with sounds. They should copy for display, and learn by heart, the one they most like.

Plenary

● Collect all the alliterative poetry lines and read and sequence them to make a class poem. The children may suggest the sequence reflects where they sit in class; putting all boys names then all the girls names together; putting names into alphabetical order; going from longest to shortest... Read the finished poem together.
● Ask a few children to show and read their other poems, explaining their choice of text and decisions about layout.

Football and other favourites

Objectives

NLS
T7: To select, prepare, read aloud and recite by heart poetry that plays with language or entertains.

S&L
29 Speaking: To choose and prepare poems for performance.

What you need
● Photocopiable page 168
● selection of poetry anthologies
● the children's own collections of favourite poems.

Shared text-level work
● Ask the children to read 'How to Score Goals' to themselves and then read it aloud in pairs.
● Help the children to appreciate that each verse gives a different devious method of goal scoring!
● Then encourage volunteers to read a verse each to the class. Discuss what made the various readings effective. For example, the use of different tones of voice, pauses, pace, eye contact and actions.
● Ask the children whether they liked the poem, and why or why not. Which verse did they think funniest? Note different favourites and explain that it is good to have different opinions about a poem because we are all individuals. All readers think in different ways and have different interests, responses and preferences.

Guided and independent work
● Explain to the children that you want them to work in pairs to write two additional verses for the poem, suggesting other ways to deceive the goalkeeper.
● Again, encourage them to practise saying these verses aloud. How do they sound? Do they fit nicely with the original?
● Let the children look through the poetry books for one poem they particularly like. Explain that this can be any sort of poem at all - anything that takes their fancy.
● Ask the children to read the poem several times to themselves and once to their partner. Ask them to explain why they like it, and identify the two or three lines they like best.
● Now teach the children one way to memorise a poem. Tell them to read their poem through until they reach a particularly striking or memorable image or couple of lines. They should try to remember these first. Then suggest they read and remember the lines immediately before or after these lines (whichever makes best sense). Tell them to say all four lines, and then choose a further two lines to remember. Children will probably not have time to memorise the whole poem in class, and should finish this for homework.
● Once they have made a good attempt at remembering the whole poem, they should copy it out for their personal anthologies and write about which lines they learned first, and why.

Differentiation

Less able
● Children will benefit from adult support and encouragement to find and learn a suitable poem.

More able
● Children should be encouraged to choose longer and more challenging poems.

Plenary
● Ask each child to choose one of their goal-scoring verses. Select eight children to come to the front and perform their verses to the class, making an eight-verse poem.
● Ask other children to read or recite their favourite poem and explain how they went about learning it.
● Choose some of the poems for the poetry wall.

Limerick muddle

Part A

◼ The lines of these limericks have been muddled up. Can you sort them out?

Heartbeat Chartbeat

There once were five patients from Barts
With irregular beats to their hearts;
And, with pleasure, they found
That they reached Number One in the Charts!
They recorded the sound

Trevor Harvey

There once was a teacher from Crewe

There once was a teacher from Crewe
They had 'spellings' galore –
And when they were done, they said 'PHEW!'
There once was a teacher from Crewe
SIXTEEN HUNDRED AND FOUR!
Who gave her class too much to do;

Trevor Harvey

Part B

◼ Opposite are two limericks that have been muddled up together. Can you separate them and put the lines in the right order?

Clue: Find the first lines of each poem, and then the second lines. Use the rhyme pattern to find the final lines. Then sort out the middle two lines that make sense and rhyme for each poem.

There Once Was A Young Boy Called Garth
There Once Was A Young Girl Called Jane

Now, when he goes out, people laugh!
Who wore all his clothes in the bath,
That his trousers would shrink.
But she did it TWICE-
There once was a young girl called Jane
There once was a young boy called Garth
Who flew round the room like a plane.
Now, ONCE was not nice,
For the boy didn't think
Then again and AGAIN and AGAIN!

Trevor Harvey

Part C

◼ Have a go at writing your own limerick.

I met a young girl/boy named ___
Who was ___
When she/he ___
She/he ___
That ___ young girl/boy named __

TERM 3

Adventures of Isabel

Isabel met an enormous bear,

Isabel, Isabel, didn't care;

The bear was hungry, the bear was ravenous,

The bear's big mouth was cruel and cavernous.

The bear said, Isabel, glad to meet you,

How do, Isabel, now I'll eat you!

Isabel, Isabel, didn't worry,

Isabel didn't scream or scurry.

She washed her hands and she straightened her hair up

Then Isabel quietly ate the bear up.

Ogden Nash

The Story of Augustus

Augustus was a chubby lad;

Fat ruddy cheeks Augustus had;

And everybody saw with joy

The plump and hearty healthy boy.

He ate and drank as he was told,

And never let his soup get cold.

But one day , one cold winter's day,

He scream'd out – 'Take the soup away!

O take the nasty soup away!

I won't have any soup today.'

Next day, now, the picture shows

How lank and lean Augustus grows!

Yet, though he feels so weak and ill,

The naughty fellow cries out still –

'Not any soup for me, I say:

O take the nasty soup away!

I won't have any soup today.'

The third day comes: Oh what a sin!

To make himself so pale and thin.

Yet, when the soup is put on table,

He screams, as loud as he is able,-

'Not any soup for me, I say:

O take the nasty soup away!

I won't have any soup today.'

Look at him, now the fourth day's come!

He scarcely weighs a sugar-plum;

He's like a little bit of thread,

And on the fifth day, he was – dead!

Dr Heinrich Hoffmann

Mrs Murphy and Mrs Murphy's kids

Mrs Murphy,
   If you please,
Kept her kids,
   In a can of peas.

The kids got bigger,
   And the can filled up,
So she moved them into
   A measuring cup.

But the kids got bigger
   And the cup got crammed,
So she poured them into
   A frying pan,

But the kids grew bigger
   And the pan began to stink,
So she pitched them all
   In the kitchen sink

But the kids kept growing
   And the sink went *kaplooey* ,
So she dumped them on their ears
   In a crate of chop suey.

But the kids kept growing
   And the crate got stuck,
So she carted them away
   In a ten-ton truck.

And she said, 'Thank goodness
   I remembered that truck
Or my poor little children
   Would be out of luck!'

But the darn kids grew
   Till the truck wouldn't fit,
And she had to haul them off
   To a gravel pit.

But the kids kept growing
   Till the pit was too small,
So she bedded them down
   In a shopping mall.

But the kids grew enormous
   And the mall wouldn't do,
So she herded them together
   In an empty zoo.

But the kids grew gigantic
And the fence went *pop*!
So she towed them away
To a mountain top.

But the kids just grew
   And the mountain broke apart,
And she said, 'Darned kids,
   They were pesky from the start!'

So she waited for a year,
   And she waited for another,
And the kids grew up
   And had babies like their mother.

And Mrs Murphy's kids –
   You can think what you please –
Kept all *their* kids
   In a can of peas.

Dennis Lee

The King's Breakfast

The King asked
The Queen, and
The Queen asked
The Dairymaid:
'Could we have some butter for
The Royal slice of bread?'
The Queen asked
The Dairymaid,
The Dairymaid
Said, 'Certainly,
I'll go and tell
The cow
Now
Before she goes to bed.'

The Dairymaid
She curtsied,
And went and told
The Alderney:
'Don't forget the butter for
The Royal slice of bread.'
The Alderney
Said sleepily:
'You'd better tell
His Majesty
That many people nowadays
Like marmalade
Instead.'

The Dairymaid
Said 'Fancy!'
And went to
Her Majesty.
She curtsied to the Queen, and
She turned a little red:
'Excuse me,
Your Majesty,
For taking of
The liberty,
But marmalade is tasty, if
It's very

Thickly
Spread.'

The Queen said
'Oh!'
And went to
His Majesty:
'Talking of the butter for
The Royal slice of bread,
Many people
Think that
Marmalade
Is nicer.
Would you like to try a little
Marmalade
Instead?'

The King said,
'Bother!'
And then he said,
'Oh, deary me!'
 The King sobbed, 'Oh, deary me!'
And went back to bed.
'Nobody,'
He whimpered,
'Could call me
A fussy man;
I *only* want
A little bit
Of butter for
My bread!'

The Queen said,
'There, there!'
And went to
The Dairymaid.
The Dairymaid,
Said, 'There there!'
And went to the shed.
The cow said
'There, there!
I didn't really
Mean it;
Here's milk for his porringer
And butter for his bread.'

The Queen took
The butter
And brought it to
His Majesty;
The King said,
'Butter, eh?'
And bounced out of bed.
'Nobody,' he said,
As he kissed her
Tenderly,
'Nobody,' he said,
As he slid down
The banisters,
'Nobody,
My darling,
Could call me
A fussy man –
BUT
I do like a little bit of butter to my
bread!'

A. A. Milne

Writing funny poems

An attempt at unrhymed verse

People tell you all the time
Poems do not have to rhyme.
It's often better if they don't
And I'm determined this one won't
               Oh dear.

Never mind, I'll start again.
Busy, busy with my pen . . . cil
I can do it if I try –
Easy, peasy, pudding and gherkins

Writing verse is so much fun,
Cheering as the summer weather,
Makes you feel alert and bright,
'Specially when you get it more or
    less the way you want it.

Wendy Cope

The Tutor

A tutor who tooted the flute
Tried to teach two young tooters to toot,
Said the two to the Tutor,
"Is it harder to toot, or
To tutor two tooters to toot?"

Carolyn Wells

A Fly and a Flea in a Flue

A fly and a flea in a flue
Were imprisoned, so what could they do?
Said the fly, "Let us flee!"
"Let us fly!" said the flea,
And they flew through a flaw in the flue.

Anonymous

TERM 3

How to Score Goals

(1)
Approach with ball
Point left
Say, 'Ooh , look – a bunny
rabbit'
Shoot right
Goal.

(2)
Approach with ball
Point right
Say, 'Ooh , look – a fiver!'
Shoot left
Goal.

(3)
Approach with ball
Say, 'Sorry about all this
trickery
I never say any rabbit!'
Offer to shake hands
Shoot.

(4)
Approach with ball
Sudden sound of bagpipes
(For this you will need an
accomplice)
Goal.

(5)
Approach with ball
Plus cake
Sing 'Happy Birthday to you!'
Invite goalie
To blow his candles out
etc.

(6)
Approach with ball
Point skywards
Say, 'Ooh , look – a vulture!'
(He will have forgotten the
rabbit by this time)
Goal.

Allan Ahlberg

UNIT 4

Authors

Children begin this week by thinking about authors as real people who have good and bad experiences, friends, worries, triumphs and jokes. They have an opportunity to research authors and to evaluate authors' web pages. Towards the middle and end of this week, the focus shifts onto the reader and children are encouraged to share their own experiences of books and to think about their own favourite books and authors. The week ends with the children writing a book review for a book that they have either loved or hated. It is helpful, but not essential, if the children are already familiar with some stories by the authors discussed in Hour 1.

Hour	Shared text-level work	Shared word-/sentence-level work	Guided and independent work	Plenary
1 Alike and different	Reading about Colin McNaughton and comparing him with themselves; organising a report.	Practising independent spelling.	Writing a short report about similarities to and differences from the author.	Reading reports; discussing new interest in the author.
2 Websites and books	Writing criteria for a good webpage.		Exploring author's web page and evaluating his/her work.	Sharing reviews and discussing works; sending reports to publishers.
3 Series authors	Identifying and researching authors of series fiction.		Writing lift-the flap book reviews to indicate what series fiction they like.	Discussing why people like particular books.
4 Book trails	Book-link game to make connections as a way of highlighting preferences.		Completing personal book trails and using them to write about preferences.	Following and examining the trails.
5 Book review	Considering elements of a persuasive book review.		Choosing a book to review and writing a review for a classmate or the headteacher.	Seeing how successful the reviews are.

Key assessment opportunities
● Can the children discuss their reading likes and dislikes?
● Are they using independent spelling strategies
● Can they write persuasive book reviews?

Alike and different

Shared text-level work

● Introduce the topic of favourite authors and books. Show the class some books by Colin McNaughton and discuss those they have read. If children are unfamiliar with the books, read one quickly to them.
● Explain that the photocopiable page about Colin McNaughton tells them all about what he is like and how he became an author-illustrator.
● Help the children to read the text, and clarify any words or phrases they do not understand.
● Tell the children that you are going to show them how to write a report on how they are each similar to and different from this famous author.
● Point out that it is important to identify key facts before writing a report. Ask the children to tell you what they now know about Colin McNaughton. As each piece of information is given, highlight it in the text or list it on the board. Discuss each idea as you go, asking children if they have similar likes, dislikes, family, experiences or feelings.
● When you have six or seven pieces of information, model how to organise them into a report. Choose one child (or use yourself) as an example and code each idea according to whether the child shares Colin McNaughton's view/experience or not. Then group the ideas to form two paragraphs, the first beginning, for example, *Colin McNaughton and I are alike in some ways. We both... However, we are also very different. For example, he... but I...*

Shared word-level work

● As you write, encourage the children to help you with spellings. Ask them to use letter strings they recognise, and to examine the features of a word to see if it looks right.

Guided and independent work

● Ask the children to use the ideas already identified, plus any others they would like to add, to write a report about how they are similar to and different from Colin McNaughton.
● Encourage children to check their work as they write and use the spelling strategies practised in shared writing.

Plenary

● Either ask some children to read their reports, or read them 'anonymously' and see if the children can guess who wrote them.
● Ask the children if they appreciate the author's work more after this investigation. Also ask them to think about Colin McNaughton as a person. Would they like him, or not, and why?
● At the end of the lesson, ask the children to suggest other authors that they would like to find out about. This will provide a good basis for Hour 2.

Websites and books

Objectives

NLS
T8: To compare and contrast works by the same author.
T9: To be aware of authors and to discuss preferences.
T17: To 'scan' indexes, directories and IT sources to locate information quickly and accurately.
S5: To learn how sentences can be joined in more complex ways through using a widening range of conjunctions.

What you need
● An author's website or publisher's author web page for demonstration (if possible from the list generated in yesterday's plenary).

Shared text-level work
● Explain that a good way to find out about authors is to look at their website or web page. Brainstorm features that a make a good web page, and list ideas on the board. Consider:

- What information would they like to read about the author?
- What activities would they like to be on the site?
- Would they like a section for 'Frequently Asked Questions'?
- Given a list of books by this author, what information would they like about each book?
- Would they like a section for readers' reviews?

● Note the different features and sections of the website. Use the class ideas of what makes a good web page to begin to evaluate it. In particular, look at the descriptions of the books. What would the children add, based on their knowledge of the books? Ask them to identify one new book they would like to read, and why.

Guided and independent work
● Depending on the children's familiarity with websites, you may choose to get the whole class to explore the web page and list of titles you have already chosen, or allow them to choose their own.
● Let pairs explore the web page and identify books they have read and those they might like to read or would not like to read.
● Explain that they are going to write a joint evaluation of the web page and the books it features.
● Explain that the evaluation must acknowledge what they learned from the page, identify the best aspects and suggest their own response to the recommended books. The first parts will be written jointly. Their personal response to the authors' books will be discussed together but written separately. The joint report will be 'assembled' at the end.
● Ask each pair to discuss and then compose a short paragraph beginning, *We learned... from this web page...*
● Then ask them to discuss the author's books they have read and books they would like to read and to write their own views: *There were some books on the web page that I liked... Some of the books that interest me are...*
● Once the sections have been written, they should be re-read and discussed before they are 'knitted' together as a response to the author's website. Explain that knitting the work together will be made easier if the language of discussion and argument is used, such as *if, so, while, though, since*, and *when*.

Differentiation
● Do not put the most and least able together, instead, try to pair children in these groups with those from the middle of the class.

Plenary
● Share the reports and use them to build a discussion about a variety of authors and books.
● Compile the reports for sending to the authors' publishers.

Series authors

Objectives

NLS
T14: To write book reviews.
T9: To be aware of authors and to discuss preferences and reasons for these.

What you need
- Collection of series-fiction books
- coloured squares (to fit four per A4 sheet)
- adhesive tape.

Shared text-level work
- Let the children look at the series fiction books you have collected. Elicit that a series is a number of books about the same characters. Authors famous for series fiction include Enid Blyton, JK Rowling, Lucy Daniels, Francesca Simon and Frank Rodgers.
- Talk about series books the children have read, who wrote them and what they thought of them. Are there some children who have never read a book from a series? Are there children who have read every book in a series? Do children who like to read series fiction always read the books in sequence?
- Discuss series books as a concept. Why do people like to read about the same characters in lots of different stories? Children often explain that they like series fiction because it is like meeting old friends, or because the reader brings knowledge of the characters, which makes the story easy to get into.

Guided and independent work
- Remind the children how to find out about a novel by reading the title and illustration, the back cover blurb and author biography and scanning the first few pages.
- In pairs, ask them to browse the collection and discuss the books in terms of two categories:

> 1. Those authors they enjoyed reading, or think they would enjoy reading. (Perhaps they have read other books in the series, or other books by this author.)
> 2. Those they did not enjoy, or think they would not enjoy reading.

- Explain that people have different opinions and partners should not expect to agree! However, they should be able to explain why they like/ dislike the characters, the chapter lengths, the illustrations, the type of plots. Explain that it is sometimes helpful to quote directly from a book to illustrate what you are saying about a book.
- Show the children how to make a lift-the-flap mini reading journal. Divide a sheet of paper into four, each section covered by a coloured flap and pick four books (across both categories) to include in the journal. Explain that on each coloured flap, they should give brief information about a book and attach it to the sheet. Under the flap, they should write which of the two categories they would place the book in, and why, creating a short review.

Differentiation

Less able
- A writing frame could support some pupils:
Name of book
This book was written by...
who (interesting point about author).
The stories are...
The main character is ...
and... (what s/he is like).

More able
- More able children should write about their books with minimal support and should be able to give several reasons for their choice, with examples from the text.

Plenary
- Discuss what the children thought of the various books, and which categories they put them into. Read some of the mini journals. What attracts some people to one author/series and not another? Has anyone ever been surprised; thought they would enjoy something and not done so or thought they were not going to like something and did?

UNIT 4 HOUR 4 Authors

Book trails

Objectives

NLS
T1: To compare different stories; to evaluate stories and justify their preferences.
T9: To be aware of authors and discuss preferences and reasons for these.

What you need

● Selection of familiar story books
● photocopiable page 176.

Differentiation

Less able
● Omit the second part of Guided and independent work or ask children to explain links orally with their partners and to help each other if they find the trail difficult.

More able
● Encourage children to write the nature of the links alongside the link line.
● Challenge them to lay their trail in a pattern, such as a spiral.

Shared text-level work

● Explain to the children that in this lesson they will be looking at one way to discuss and share books they have read, by making connections between them.
● Display photocopiable page 176 and demonstrate how the book trail works. Start by suggesting the name of a book that is familiar to most or all of the children in the class (ideally one that has come up in earlier lessons in this unit). Write in the title as the *Start story*.
● Read through the other headings on the sheet.
● Ask a child to suggest a book that links to the start book according to one of the headings. For example, if the start story is *The Firework-Maker's Daughter* by Philip Pullman, another adventure story could be *Take a Good Look* by Jacqueline Wilson.
● Encourage the child to explain the link between the two texts by making specific reference to the text where appropriate (such as the feelings generated, what makes it a similar kind of story, how they are both scary/funny/set in outer space).
● Write the title of this book, for example, *Take a Good Look* under the adventure story heading and draw an arrow to it from the start story to show the link.
● Identify the author of the story and briefly outline the plot. Discuss the characters and the setting of the story and how they both help the story to fit the chosen heading.
● Now look for another heading, for example, the same author, and a new book that links to *Take a Good Look*; perhaps *Mark Spark in the Dark*. Add an arrow as before.
● See how far you can go as a class, encouraging all of the children to contribute a suitable link. Stop when there are no more headings, or when the children cannot think of any other books.

Guided and independent work

● Ask the children to brainstorm and discuss books in pairs in order to complete their individual book trails. If possible, encourage them to only include books they have enjoyed.
● Once the trail is complete, ask the children to write a short piece to explain their book trail. The children need only write a few sentences about each book, explaining why it is suitable for that category and why they liked it enough to include it.

Plenary

● Follow and talk about the different book trails produced. What general preferences can be identified from them?
● Note any books that have come up frequently and/or have been included under different headings by different children.

Book review

Objectives

NLS
T1: To re-tell main points of a story in sequence; to evaluate stories and justify preferences.
T14: To write book reviews for a specified audience.

What you need
● Selection of familiar story books.

Shared text-level work

● Remind the children of the book reviews they wrote in Hour 3. Explain that now you want them to write a review that persuades someone to read the book. Discuss that this review needs to include a summary of the story and mention the main characters. Explain that, to write a persuasive review, they will need to think about the person they want to persuade.
● Organise the children into working pairs within two groups (see Differentiation too):

> ● Tell half the class to think of three things that the headteacher would think important when choosing to buy a book for the class.
> ● Tell the other half to think of three things that might persuade a fellow pupil to read a book.

● Write key words and phrases from their suggestions as two lists on the board. For example, a headteacher might look for: cost, durability, educational value, books to appeal to particular groups (such as boys, particular age groups). Children might look for humour, good illustrations short/long chapters, whether their friends have read it.
● Show the children a book that you know most of them have read. Briefly recap the main characters and events.
● Now tell the children to discuss in their pairs how they would review this book so that either the headteacher or the fellow pupil will read it. They will need to describe the book in a way that emphasises aspects of the characters and story most likely to appeal to the reader they want to convince.
● Invite some children to have a go at reviewing the book orally in front of the class.

Guided and independent work

● Ask the pairs to choose a book to review. Remind them to note key characters and story events as well as their personal opinions. Then ask them to think about how to tailor their review so that it will appeal specifically to either the headteacher or a classmate.
● Suggest that before discussing how to write their review, they should read the list on the board of the things that might persuade this person to buy any story book and from there decide which they can emphasise in this review.
● Ask the children to write their book reviews individually. Encourage them to add weight to their personal thoughts about the book by referring to details in the text, including short quotes.

Plenary

● Share some of the children's book reviews and discuss how persuasive they are. Encourage the headteacher to look at some and see if s/he is persuaded!

Differentiation

Less able
● Children might find it easier to write for a fellow pupil.

More able
● Children might find it more challenging to write for the headteacher.

Colin McNaughton biography

Comics, *Beano* and *Dandy* annuals, and Saturday morning cinema; these were the cultural influences of Colin McNaughton's childhood, ones which had a lasting effect on his own work. There were few books at home in Wallsend when he was growing up during the fifties and sixties.

Colin's dad worked in the shipyards and Colin was one of three children. He detested school, so much so he couldn't talk about it for years. But he had one marvellous teacher, who introduced him to a Youth Theatre, something quite new for a boy from his background. "Acting, costumes... marvellous if you've never known that kind of ability to express feelings before. It allowed me to break out of the scheme of things – where you simply follow you father into the shipyards and so on."

© Susan Pfannmuller/The Kansas City Star

Children have always recognised his talent, energy and humour. 'Crazy' is a key word: it's an element that runs through all of his work. "The older I get the more I realise that my sense of humour is exactly the same as it was when I was four years old – it hasn't changed at all!"

Extracted from Meet the Authors and Illustrators by Stephanie Nettell (1995, Scholastic Children's Books).

TERM 3

Book trails

1. Start with one story that you have enjoyed.
2. Use one of the headings to find a link between that story and another story.
3. Write the name of the new story under the heading. Draw an arrow to link the two stories.
4. Now see if you can link this story to a new book under a new heading.
5. Do this until you have used all the headings or cannot think of any more stories.

Start story: ___
Same setting as...
An adventure story like...
As hard to read as...
Illustrated like...
By the same author as...
A similar kind of story to...
Gives the same feeling as...
A series book like...
As scary as...
A funny story like...

UNIT 5

Note-taking and letters

In this unit, the children read and make notes about a school in the 1920s, making links to history work. They write letters to next year's Year 3s, explaining what they might expect. The children also write to their parents to give a personal report on their work, then they evaluate the class library and write to the headteacher to suggest how it might be developed. Finally, the children write persuasive letters to their own classmates, nominating one class member to receive an Annual Citizenship Award.

Hours 1 and 2 can be used in conjunction with Unit 18 in *Grammar for Writing*.

The children look at different spellings and revise common spelling patterns for long-vowel digraphs. This unit also covers *Progression in phonics* Step 7.

Hour	Shared text-level work	Shared word-/ sentence-level work	Guided reading/ writing	Independent work	Plenary
1 Schools then and now	Comparing school life now and in the past; annotating a text.	Practising the use of cues and reading strategies.	Choosing the four most important points to make a four-page information booklet.	Sharing booklets, discussing topics; making covers.	Matching word cards to words on the boar; identifying sounds with various spellings.
2 Letter to next year's class	Recounting events of the year in order to write a letter to next year's class.	Identifying sequence words.	Oral planning in A-B pairs for the letter.	Evaluating the letters, noting time/sequence words.	Sharing couplets; focusing on long-vowel digraphs and rhymes.
3 Letter to parents	Identifying headings for personal report to parents/carers.		Writing a first draft; using paragraphs to give coherence; editing for grammar, punctuation and spelling.	Sharing difficulties; practising spellings; sending letters home.	Reading and discussing new verses, focusing on rhyme.
4 Report on the class library	Identifying possible improvements and priorities for the class library; revising letter format.		Writing report on class library in the form of a letter; reading and commenting on another's report.	Discussing comments and proposing recommendations.	Discussing different uses of capital letters.
5 Annual Citizenship Award	Discussing good citizenship; shared writing of nomination.		Writing individual nominations; identifying good and bad points in partners' work.	Reading out nominations; voting and holding award ceremony.	Sharing poems, focusing on spelling and discussing how punctuation affects reading.

Key assessment opportunities
- Have the children used conventions in writing letters?
- Can they write appropriately to a specific audience?
- Are they using sequence words to help structure recounts?
- Have they identified successes and any bad points during the year?
- Can they comment constructively on each other's work?

Schools then and now

Objectives

NLS

T25: To revise and extend work on note-making from previous term.
T26: To summarise in writing the content of a passage or text and the main point it is making.
S1: To use awareness of grammar to decipher new or unfamiliar words.
S6: To investigate through reading and writing how words and phrases can signal time sequences.

What you need

● Photocopiable page 183
● zig-zag booklets made from A4 paper
● books about schools in the past (for more able children).

Shared text-level work

● Tell the children that schools have changed a lot in the last 100 years. Read the recount on the photocopiable sheet.
● Now ask the children to read the text paragraph by paragraph. Suggest that as they read, they should stop and write in the margin a few words about what they are learning. Model this if necessary.

Shared sentence-level work

● Remind the children how to work out unfamiliar words when reading. For example, words like *roasting* or *freezing* might be worked out from context and general meaning. Words like *punished* or *pockets* might need to be sounded out. Encourage children to sound out the first syllable and then use the meaning cues to guess at the whole word, quickly cross-checking that their guess was correct.

Guided and independent work

● Remind the children that to plan a report to compare this school with their own they must identify possible topics to write about.
● Demonstrate how single-word notes can help them to plan the report.
● Show the children how to go through their notes and select three one-word topic headings (one per page on the zig-zag book, leaving the front page free for the title).
● Explain how a one-word heading at the top of each page prepares the reader for the information on that page and will also help them to structure their writing. Tell the children to choose one of their key words as a topic and title for the first page in their book. Each page should tell the reader what schools were like 100 years ago and what they are like now.
● The first sentence should introduce the subject of the report and give one or two key pieces of information about it. Further sentences can elaborate on this. Discuss how it helps the reader separate paragraphs to describe what schools were like 100 years ago and what they are like now. Introduce key words and phrases such as *100 years ago... Nowadays, my school...* Children may also find terms such as *then, after, when, from* and *where* useful for this writing, and these should be displayed on the board.
● Tell the children that illustrations can be used to add visual appeal and/or to help the reader understand certain aspects of the report.

Differentiation

Less able
● Children may find it helpful to do illustrations first, using this as thinking time to prepare for their writing.

More able
● Encourage children to research more details to include in their reports.

Plenary

● Show and read some of the booklets. Discuss the topics the children chose to cover, and why.
● Consider possible titles for the booklets and ideas for cover images. Let the children choose their title and illustrate the cover as a homework task.

Objectives

NLS
T20: To write letters linked to work in other subjects; to communicate within school, selecting style and vocabulary appropriate to the intended reader.
T23: To organise letters into simple paragraphs.
S6: To investigate through reading and writing how words and phrases can signal time sequences.

S&L
33 Speaking: To sustain conversation, explaining or giving reasons for their views or choices.

Letter to next year's class

Shared text- and sentence-level work

● Explain to the children that you would like to know their thoughts about this year. Discuss the differences they found between Year 2 and Year 3 and suggest that next year's class might appreciate a preview of what they might be doing during the year.

● Review some of the main events and topics studied during the year. Encourage the children to identify interesting details and advice. Model appropriate words and phrases to signal time sequence, including *first, then, after, during, while*.

● Emphasise to the children that they should write about to or three of their own highlights that they remember best or about what they think will be most helpful for others to know. The general time words and phrases on the board will help them to put the key events in sequence.

● Remind the children that good letters include interesting, clear descriptions and personal ideas, so they should choose those events about which they have most to say.

● Recap the format of a letter and the use of the second person. Discuss how the writers might introduce and explain the topic. Remind them from their work in the previous lesson that each new topic requires a new paragraph and that this will help to break up their letter and make it more readable.

Guided and independent work

● Give the children a few minutes to choose their topics and rehearse to themselves what they want to say. Then put them into A–B pairs and ask the children labelled A to tell their B partners as much as possible about what they will write in their letter. Then ask the partners to switch roles.

● Ask all the B children to sit down and the A children to stand. Tell the children labelled A to move and find a new B partner, and to retell their letter content, this time adding more detail. Swap roles as before.

● Explain to the children that this oral rehearsal acts as both a plan and first draft for their letter and should have been helpful in fixing the language and level of formality they will use (as their letters are being written to children similar to themselves). Tell the children they should now write their letters.

Plenary

● Ask volunteers to read out their letters. Encourage the class to comment on what made each one interesting. Discuss whether the letters need redrafting, or could be sent as they are to next year's class.

● As you re-read a couple of letters aloud to the children, challenge the them to pick out time words.

Differentiation

Less able
● An introductory phrase such as *I am writing to you because...* should help struggling writers to get started

More able
● Children should write at greater length and provide more detailed and vivid descriptions. They should re-read their work independently.

TERM 3

Letter to parents

Objectives

NLS
T16: To read examples of letters written for a range of purposes.
T22: To experiment with recounting the same event in a variety of ways.
W5: To identify mis-spelt words in own writing and learn to spell them.

What you need

• Letters to parents and carers about school issues
• photocopiable page 184.

Shared text-level work

• Explain that Year 2 pupils are not the only people interested in what happens during Year 3. Parents will have had reports about the children's progress, but would also like to hear their children's views about what they have achieved.
• Suggest to the children that they write to their parents and carers. Because this is a report in the form of a letter, it will be planned under headings like the report they wrote about school now and in the past in Hour 1. Use examples from the letters to parents to explain that each paragraph deals with a new topic (and may have a subheading).
• Discuss suitable headings for their report and write suggestions (such as the various curriculum subject areas, sport, extra-curricular activities, playground and lunchtime games) on the board. As with the report in Hour 1, they should choose the headings most appropriate to them. Advise them to think about what they want to tell their parents, and what their parents would like to hear (which may be different!).
• To help with this, take the adult perspective and discuss what parents might want to know about their children, for example:

> • whether their child enjoys the subject
> • whether they work hard
> • any triumphs or high points
> • any difficulties
> • some of the important things learned the during the year.

• Write these up as prompts on the board.
• Remind the children of the layout of a letter –the address, date, greeting and so on. Explain that the first paragraph should give a brief outline of the topic and why the letter has been written.
• Show photocopiable page 184 and point out how each paragraph deals with a different game but each game is discussed in broadly similar terms.

Guided and independent work

• Allow the children to select and sequence headings for their own letter, and to write a first draft.
• Encourage the use of independent spelling strategies. Once written, the letter should be carefully checked and edited to ensure correct punctuation and that high-frequency words are correctly spelled. If appropriate, ask the children to swap their letters with their partners to check each other's spelling, grammar and punctuation.

Plenary

• Encourage comments about things that the children found difficult about writing their letters. It is likely that they had to consider not just what to say, but how to say it. How were these solved?
• Ask the children to practise spelling any mis-spelled words, and send the letters home.

Differentiation

Less able
• Ensure children have access to the prompt questions, and demonstrate how they might help them to structure their writing and generate ideas.

More able
• Encourage more able children to write independently, referring to the prompts only at the end as an aid to evaluation.

UNIT 5 HOUR 4 ▶ Note-taking and letters

TERM 3

Report on the class library

Objectives

NLS
T16: To read examples of letters; to understand form and layout including use of paragraphs, ways of starting, ending etc, and ways of addressing different audiences.
T23: To organise letters into simple paragraphs.
W19: To build up handwriting speed, fluency and legibility through practice.

Shared text-level work

● Tell the children that you would also welcome some feedback about the classroom. In particular you would like to know about the strengths and weaknesses of the library, and how it could be improved next year.
● Ask the children: Do they think it has a good selection of books for all interests – boys as well as girls? Are there too few books? Is it well organised? Is it in the best location? Have the children had any difficulties using it? Do they have enough access to it? Is there a way to make it more comfortable? Is it warm and well-lit? Are there enough chairs? Are there any books that should be thrown away – either because they are damaged or because no one reads them anymore?
● Tell the children that they will be writing a brief letter to the headteacher reporting on the library.
● Brainstorm possible headings, recalling the discussion above, and ask the children to recap on how to write their report in the form of a letter (for example, salutation; brief introduction; report text with each new topic as a new paragraph, perhaps with subheadings, closing comment and sign off).
● Remind the children that as their reader is the headteacher they will need to keep the tone polite and reasonably formal and their handwriting neat. Ask how they start the letter. For example:

> Dear Mrs Moore
> I have enjoyed using the library this year. It has some very good books. I thought you might like to know about some ideas we have had to improve it...

Guided and independent work

● Ask the children to write their letters. As this is the third report (and the second letter) this week, most of the children should be able to do this quite independently.
● Then collect all the reports and randomly redistribute them amongst the class. Ask each child to read the report they have been given. What reaction does the letter provoke in them? Do they agree with it? Do they think it is well-expressed? Are the suggested changes to the library good ones? Are they possible/practical?
● Ask the children to write a brief comment to their letter, giving their own views about any of the issues identified as well as the recommendations for improvement.

Differentiation

Less able
● Children needing support may benefit from a group discussion of the different ways to start their letter.

More able
● Encourage children to give detailed, reasoned responses to the letter they read.

Plenary

● Read out some of the letters and the responses to the children.
● If reports raise issues of school policy, or make recommendations that are either simple to implement or, by contrast, have financial implications, more able children could perhaps write an additional letter to combine these helpful suggestions and send it to the headteacher.

Annual Citizenship Award

Objectives

NLS
T20: To write letters linked to work in other subjects.
T21: To use IT to bring to a published form.
T23: To organise letters into simple paragraphs.

S&L
33 Speaking: To sustain conversation, explaining or giving reasons for their views or choices.

What you need
● Photographs of the children.

Shared text-level work

● Introduce the Annual Citizenship Award that will be given to one child in the class. Tell the children that they will all write letters of nomination and then vote to decide who should receive the award.
● Discuss what a person might do to deserve the award. Emphasise that being talented or popular is not enough; good citizens use their talents or popularity to benefit others, particularly in places like the playground. Brainstorm what makes a good citizen, for example, helpful, kind, truthful, share their things, patient. In the playground, a good citizen will be good fun and include others in games, make people feel good about themselves, be fair and stick up for those in trouble. If appropriate, talk about some famous people the children think are good citizens, and why.
● Model how to write a nomination letter by asking the children to choose a member of staff that they think deserves an award; perhaps a teacher, classroom assistant, playground supervisor, cook, secretary. Model a suitable opening sentence (see suggestion in Differentiation). Ask the children to identify one quality that makes this person a good citizen. Then ask for one or two examples of this during the year.
● Organise this information with one quality, the reason why it is important and examples of it in action, per paragraph.

Guided and independent work

● Ask the children to look around the class (remind them of any absent pupils) and to identify (just to themselves) one person whom they believe has consistently been a good citizen in the past year. Then, ask them to think of this person's qualities and to think of evidence of this that would convince others of their worth.
● Tell them to write their letters as modelled in shared work.
● Explain that all the nomination letters will be displayed alongside photographs of the nominee and nominator.
● Ask the children to read their draft letters to their writing partners. The writing partner should identify one really good, persuasive sentence and suggest one way in which the letter might be improved. Authors should consider their writing partners' comments before redrafting.
● Help at least one group to scan the photographs and publish them with their typed letters. Encourage them to maintain the letter format and choose an attractive font.

Plenary

● Ask the children to read their letters to the class to persuade others to vote for their nominee.
● Once the vote has been held, you may like to hold an award ceremony. Post nominees and winners on the school website.

Differentiation

Less able
● Suggest an opening sentence such as *Dear friends, I think XXXXX deserves to win the award because...*

More able
● Encourage more able children to provide several reasons and examples to support their nomination.

School in the 1920s

Sam is nine years old. His great-grandmother is over 100. On her 100th birthday she got a card from the Queen and a birthday cake from the Mayor. One of the things that Sam likes is to listen to his great-grandmother talking about her life when she was young. Sometimes he can hardly believe how different things were in those days. Here is a story his great-grandmother told him about when her brother went to school.

"When my little brother went to school there were over 50 children in a class. The teacher sat at her table at the front. She had a class helper who was an older girl – she would have been about 13. She taught the children like my brother, who couldn't read very well. There was a big fire at the front of the classroom and the caretaker used to come and add more coal every few hours. It was roasting at the front of the class and freezing at the back. The children sat on long benches and my little brother usually sat near the back because he wasn't very good at reading and writing. Everyone sat according to who came top in the class test and the best readers were always at the front. If you were a good reader, you were always nice and warm!

"My little brother only had one pair of school trousers and one pair of shoes and when it snowed and it was freezing cold our mum used to give my brothers hot baked potatoes to put in their pockets. The potato warmed their hands on the long walk to school – it was four miles – and then they ate it for lunch! There were no school lunches in those days.

"The teacher was very strict and work had to be done in silence. In those days teachers used to smack children across the hands with a cane or a leather strap if they were naughty. My little brother was caned when he was late or when he didn't understand or if he moved or talked. He had to move sometimes because his hands and legs were cold.

"At playtime he'd play in the school yard. It was quite rough and muddy. The toilets were in an outside shed at the bottom of the yard. When playtime was finished the teacher rang a big bell and everyone had to get into lines."

TERM 3

Dear Thom...

Dear Thom

I thought you might be interested in knowing how I am getting along with the computer games you lent me. I've had good fun playing all the games. Some are easier than others. I also like some of them more than others.

One of the games I like best is SSX Tricky. This is just brilliant! It took me a while to remember how to select and control the skiers, but now I really enjoy deciding which short cuts to aim for on the course. At first, my skier kept falling and I came last all the time. Then, I realised how to use short cuts and not try doing tricks all the time. Re-starting the race was handy too if I was well behind! My brother still has to help me out sometimes, but I think this game has been particularly good for my control skills!

A very different game that I am enjoying is The Sims. It takes me ages to distribute my 25 points, and I know that I will never create one person who is absolutely perfect in every way, but this game taught me a lot. The most important thing it taught me was to READ ALL THE INSTRUCTIONS!

Another game I like is the FIFA football game. I enjoyed choosing my teams and I have learned to read the games better, making sure all my players are in the right positions. I even think it has helped me as a football player in real life.

Well, those are just three of the games. I'll return all the games later this week. Thanks for letting me have a go at them.

Best wishes

Sam

PS. I think it would be a good idea if computer games were in the National Curriculum, don't you? Shall we write to the Prime Minister to suggest this?

UNIT 6

Alphabetical text

In this unit, the children are introduced to different types of guide books and directories and learn how they are organised by making their own versions. They write entries, and put them into alphabetical order to create class publications of a guide to class skills, a topic reference finder and a good read guide, which could be sold to parents on parents' evening. The children also learn how the school library is organised and use a library trail task to assess how effectively they use it.

Hour	Shared text-level work	Shared word-/ sentence-level work	Guided reading/ writing	Independent work	Plenary
1 A guide to skills in class	Examining how a directory is organised and used and the different types of entries.	Exploring use of commas in lists.	Designing class directory entries; organising them alphabetically.	Publishing and using the directory.	Matching word cards to words on the board; identifying sounds with various spellings.
2 The library trail	Considering how the library is used and organised.		Completing a book-trail challenge in pairs.	Discussing what children noticed about their partners' knowledge of the library.	Sharing couplets; focusing on long-vowel digraphs and rhymes.
3 Library posters	Examining posters to generate criteria for clear instructions.		Creating information posters/fliers to help younger children to use the library.	Evaluating the posters in terms of evaluation criteria.	Reading and discussing new verses, focusing on rhyme.
4 The Good Read Guide	Examining structure and uses of listings guides to, for example, hotels, restaurants.		Writing entries for highly recommended books and books about which the writers are ambivalent; sorting entries alphabetically.	Saying why an entry is effective; publishing the 'Good read guide' for parents' evening.	Discussing different uses of capital letters.
5 A topic reference finder	Determining appropriate headings for a topic reference book/directory; revising use of contents and index pages.		Collecting and collating information pages for different topic headings; sorting them alphabetically.	Discussing strategies used for locating items in alphabetical sequence.	Sharing poems, focusing on spelling and discussing how punctuation affects reading.

Key assessment opportunities
● Can children explain how the layout and wording of a short information or persuasive text influences the reader?
● Are they using commas to separate items in a list?
● Can they locate items in alphabetical sequence?
● Do they recognise different ways to use the library and how it is organised?

Objectives

NLS
T21: To use IT to bring to a published form – discuss relevance of layout, font to audience.
T24: To make alphabetically ordered texts.
S7: To become aware of the use of commas in marking grammatical boundaries within sentences.

What you need

● Local directory such as *Yellow Pages*
● examples of good and poor use of layout, font and punctuation in entries in the directory.

A guide to skills in class

Shared text- and sentence-level work

● Show the class the directory. Explain its alphabetical organisation within categories and discuss why and how directories like this are used. Let children see a few of the pages to see the range of entries.
● Suggest that it would be a good idea to have a class directory listing the special talents of all class members. Some children might be brilliant with animals such as walking dogs or cleaning out hamster cages. Others might want to advertise their skills on a particular computer game, or be particularly good at entertaining a younger brother or sister or at sports, art, music or crafts.
● Tell the children to think of three or four different skill areas they could offer as their own entries in the class directory. They will need to make the entries as different from each other as possible.
● Explain that although the entries need to be organised in a uniform way, with the surnames first, some may be 'line' entries and others may be small adverts. Illustrate this with examples from the directory.
● Give the children some pages from the directory to read so they can see how the adverts promote the companies' services in different ways.
● Discuss examples that illustrate good and poor use of persuasive language, layout, fonts and punctuation, including commas.
● Point out that effective entries often contain a list of all the services that are offered and a comma separates each service in the list if they are within a sentence.

Guided and independent work

● Ask the children to write and design their directory entries, using IT where possible. Encourage a mixture of both boxed advertisements and line entries.
● Now gather the children together, collect all their topics, and discuss suitable classification headings to use. Write these on the board. (You may want to record how many entries you are getting for each heading as you do this.) Ask the children to help you to sequence these categories alphabetically.
● Collect up all the entries for each category. Give pairs of children all the entries for one or two categories to organise into alphabetical order.

Plenary

● Share the work and show how the entries will be cut and pasted into a published format within their classifications. This can be done by hand or by using IT. Ask the children to explain to the class how they will then look up particular entries in the new directory.
● Children may like to invent some 'dictionary work' questions or activities to use on the finished directories.

Differentiation

Less able
● Give less able children slightly smaller categories to handle when collating entries.

More able
● Encourage more able children to include persuasive wording in their adverts.

The library trail

Objectives

NLS
T17: To 'scan' indexes etc to locate information quickly and accurately.
T18: To locate books by classification in class or school libraries.

S&L
25 Speaking: To explain a process or present information.

What you need
● Photocopiable page 191
● clipboards
● access to the school library.

Shared text-level work
● Find out from the children when and how they first learned to use the school library.
● Ask them to think about the different ways in which the school library is used. For example, sometimes they need to find a particular book in the fiction or non-fiction section. At other times, they need to find out about a topic, but do not have a specific book in mind or they want to browse to choose a fiction book to read.
● Explain that each of the tasks in this lesson will entail using the library in a different way.
● Ask the children to talk in pairs about when they last used the library and what they did.
● Discuss the importance of understanding how the library is organised, and being able to use this knowledge to use it in different ways. Talk about occasions when the children have found it difficult to use the library, and how they overcame these difficulties.
● Use these discussions to establish how the school library is organised and remind the children about how to use the classification system and alphabetical order to find appropriate books.

Guided and independent work
● Explain to the children that you are going to give them a book trail challenge, to be done in pairs.
● Children within each pair should take it in turns to attempt each challenge and observe each other, reporting back on how directly/easily the challenge was completed.
● Distribute the photocopiable sheets and answer any questions the children may have about the tasks or how to observe their partner.
● Before you organise the pairs, offer to hold a further five-minute mini-tutorial to revise in more detail how the school library is organised. Allow children to opt into this tutorial if they feel they would benefit from it before attempting the book trail challenge. Pupils who do not need the tutorial can be put into pairs and begin work.
● To avoid parts of the library becoming overcrowded, you will probably want to start each pair off at a different point on the challenge. Each column contains similar tasks, however the early tasks for Partner A are slightly easier than those for Partner B. Responses should be recorded on a separate piece of paper.

Differentiation

Less able
● Give less able children fewer tasks to complete on the photocopiable sheet.

More able
● More able children and those who finish quickly can be asked to invent their own tasks for a future library trail.

Plenary
● Ask the children to present their feedback about their partners. Which tasks did they find easy and hard? What did they notice about their partner's knowledge of the library?
Ask if the children found out any more about the library and if they will now find it easier to use. Did they find any interesting books?

Library posters

Objectives

NLS
T18: To locate books by classification in class or school libraries.
T21: To use IT to bring to a published form – discuss relevance of layout, font etc. to audience.

What you need
● Examples of information posters, if possible

Shared text-level work

● Remind the children that we often use the library to answer different kinds of questions. Explain that younger pupils may appreciate some helpful posters to show them the best way to use the library to find:

- a fiction book they might enjoy reading
- a particular fiction book or author they know they want to read
- a non-fiction book by a particular author
- a non-fiction book that will answer specific questions about a topic.

● Ask the children to examine the information posters you have brought to show them, explaining in which context they would appear, as appropriate. Point out that each poster is designed to give instructions and helpful advice. Using the poster examples, and others the children think of, make a list of the features that make each information poster most helpful. The children may suggest:

- clear headings with key words
- flow charts
- questions
- short, succinct instructions
- numbered or bulleted points
- pictures and diagrams
- colourful presentation.

● Revisit the information posters and use these headings to discuss what makes them effective, or not.

Guided and independent work

● Split the class into four groups and ask the children to work in pairs to draft a poster that will help others use the library effectively for one of the purposes listed above. First, they should discuss the information that their poster needs to convey. Then they should plan the layout and text of their poster and decide the headings to use; what to say, and how to say it; whether to use pictures, diagrams, arrows or flow charts; the layout, fonts and colours they want to use. Remind them to consider their young audience when discussing these points.
● Encourage children to experiment with word-processing and desktop publishing programs to publish their posters. For larger displays, A4 posters can be photocopied to A3.

Plenary

● Display the posters and evaluate them against the criteria generated at the start of the lesson. Children could take their posters to a younger class and ask them for comments.
● Display the posters in the library, either on the wall, or as A4 fliers. They could also be put into a folder and used to form a general information book.

Differentiation

Less able
● Some children may particularly benefit from discussion to ensure that they are clear about the key points.

More able
● Children should focus on putting information across in a succinct and clear way. Aim for a balance between a clear explanation, with good layout and the right amount of text.

The good read guide

Objectives

NLS
T14: To write book reviews for a specified audience.
T24: To make alphabetically ordered texts.

What you need
● Examples of guides to good hotels or good restaurants.

Shared text-level work
● Show the class the guide books you have collected. Discuss why people use these guides, and explore how they are organised.
● Suggest that it would be helpful to produce a 'Good read guide', aimed particularly at children of their own age group and younger.
● Explain that the guide should contain all sorts of books and that it is important to be truthful about them.
● Look at how the features, organisation and the layout of the guides help the reader. Highlight features such as alphabetical organisation of entries (by name), the star ratings and how the written text is structured in terms of a short description of the place followed by a few sentences about the sort of people to whom it might appeal.
● Discuss how symbols like this could be used to indicate an overall rating for a book, but discuss other aspects that will need to be indicated in a simple graphic way (a key): the type of book (fiction/ non fiction) or story (adventure, funny and so on), whether it might appeal mostly to boys or girls or both, a rough age group; how difficult or quick it is to read; how long it is.
● Explain that symbols can help to save on space and are easy to use at a glance, but that too many symbols can be confusing for the reader; sometimes a phrase or sentence is more user-friendly.
● Ask the children to suggest a book they have read recently and work together to begin writing an entry for it. Decide as a class which symbols to use.

Guided and independent work
● Ask the children to write two entries: one for a book that they would highly recommend and one for a book about which they are more ambivalent. They should use the text structures and symbols that have been agreed.
● Remind the childen of their audience and that the guide will be published for sale.
● Once finished, ask the children to take responsibility for one part of the alphabet (a–d; e–h and so on), collect the relevant titles and organise them alphabetically.

Plenary
● Ask the children to find one good entry from these they have been putting in sequence, and to explain what is good about it.
● In a follow-up lesson, compile and publish the guide, ideally using IT and checking all spellings and sentences. Children may like to sell their 'Good read guide' on parents' night, with proceeds going to charity.

Differentiation
● Give more able pupils those sections of the alphabet that have more titles to organise, and less able pupils those parts with fewer.

A topic reference finder

Objectives

NLS
T17: To 'scan' indexes etc to locate information quickly and accurately.
T21: Use IT to bring to a published form.
T24: to make alphabetically ordered texts.

What you need
● Topic reference books.

Shared text-level work
● Ask the children what they do if they want to find out about a particular aspect of a topic. Some will automatically ask for help. Others will flick through a book, looking at the pictures until they come across something relevant. Most will use the contents and index to look up relevant words. They should be able to tell you that if a word is not listed, they will try a synonym.
● Explain that it would be useful to have another reference book – one that told them exactly where they could go to find out more about particular aspects of a topic. This would save the children time and mean that they were not taking books out of the library that they ended up not needing.
● Ask the children what information might be useful (apart from the author, book title, page number). Perhaps some brief notes and/or a star rating system.
● Brainstorm the different aspects of a current class topic that the children might want to read about in more depth. Aim for about four to eight headings.
● Take one heading and demonstrate how to use the index and contents pages of one book to locate relevant information about that heading. Show the class how to write the author, book title, page number and notes to indicate their evaluation of the information and how it is presented.

Guided and independent work
● Organise the children into groups of three or four. Ask each child to write each heading on a separate sheet of paper. Give each group a few topic books. Ask everyone to take one book each and locate information for as many of the headings as they can. When they find appropriate information, they should record the author, book title, page number, and their own evaluation as appropriate.
● When the groups have four or five entries under each heading, ask each child to collect the sheets for one heading and to put the entries into alphabetical order by author. They should check with their group to ensure that they have sequenced the authors correctly.
● Help the children to enter and organise this data onto the computer, ensuring that they locate their own entries in correct alphabetical sequence within the whole class list.

Differentiation

Less able
● Help children to note their evaluations in simple form.

More able
● More able children could be responsible for alphabetising more than one sheet.

Plenary
● Display the final publication. Discuss the strategies to use for locating items in alphabetical order. Do the children visualise that part of the alphabet, recite the alphabet from scratch until they reach the appropriate letter, or recite the alphabet from an appropriate point? Which is more effective, and why?
● Keep the directory available for use during topic work.

Book trail challenge

◀ Take it in turns to complete the challenge below.

◀ Watch carefully as your partner completes each task. Does your partner go straight to the correct section? What does s/he do to find a particular book? Does s/he show a good understanding of how the library is organised?

Partner A	Partner B
Find three good books about sea animals. Write down the names of the authors.	Find a book that can explain all the different parts of a castle. Write down the title, author, chapter and page numbers.
Find the section just before space and the planets. What is it about?	Find a fiction book written by an author whose name begins with *St*. Write down the author's full name and the book title.
Find a book that can explain how and why the Ancient Egyptians made mummies. Write down the title, author, chapter and page numbers.	Find a poetry book written or edited by a poet that you have enjoyed reading this year.
Find a fiction book that might interest a girl of about six years old.	Find three interesting books about living in another country. Write down the names of the authors.
Find a fiction book written by an author whose name begins with *Ki*. Write down the author's full name and book title.	Find the section straight after the human body. What is it about?
Find a poetry book of funny poems. Write down the title and author/ editor.	Find a fiction book that would be enjoyed by an eight-year-old boy.